I heard this in the Spirit this very night that this place [Discovery Camp] was born and brought into manifestation in the natural, physical world straight from the heart of the Father God.

—KENNETH COPELAND
Founder, Kenneth Copeland Ministries
Spoken during a dedication service at
Discovery Camp on January 23, 2004

I highly recommend Rachel's book. One of our daughters and spiritual sons were tremendously blessed by their experiences of Discovery Camp.

—TAFFI DOLLAR
Cofounder, World Changers Church International
Atlanta, Georgia

In these days where many are looking at natural circumstances, Rachel Burchfield teaches us to look up—not down! Every believer should read this book and then keep it to use in their personal devotions year after year. One simply cannot read a single chapter without leaving its pages rejoicing. This book is a page-turner!

—CINDY JACOBS
Generals International

Rachel Burchfield is an amazing and very talented woman of God. She teaches the Word of God with great authority and has written a book that will bless multitudes. I salute her.

—DODIE OSTEEN
Cofounder, Lakewood Church
Houston, Texas

God has given tremendous insight to my friend and colleague in ministry, Rachel Burchfield, in her book *Miracle Moments*. Her theology on the timing of God, the revelation of dreams, using God's Word as the source for instruction for life, and using our faith to overcome are not only heartwarming but also resourceful for the Christian who seeks the Christ-centered relationship.

—Stanley F. Seat, PLLE, CPA, CFF, CIRA, JD, DMin

Rachel's refreshing book, highlighting the remarkable history of Discovery Camp, motivates us all to dream big and believe for our own miracle moments. I can testify firsthand what an awesome impact Tommy and Rachel have had upon many youth and Christian leaders. Rachel, ever-inspiring Bible teacher, shares personal gems throughout the book. I especially liked her teaching on finding joy amid our trials. Let *Miracle Moments* release the miracle of hope into your heart!

—Quin Sherrer
Author, *A Mother's Guide to Praying for Your Children*

Only Rachel would describe a half-million campers as an adventure! We wholeheartedly recommend this book and have been personally inspired by the Burchfields' visionary leadership for twenty-five years. You will find great wisdom on marriage, parenting, and leadership from a team who not only preach it well but also live it out beautifully.

—Casey and Wendy Treat
Copastors, Christian Faith Center
Seattle, Washington

God still performs miracles! He positions His people so they can experience miracles as they pursue His destiny for their lives. Rachel Burchfield's powerful book *Miracle Moments* causes alertness to these supernatural manifestations. She brings understanding to the process of preparation for miracles to occur. God's plan for you is a life filled with miracles. Read this book with expectancy in your heart. Then don't miss your miracle moment!

—BARBARA WENTROBLE
President, International Breakthrough Ministries
Author, *Prophetic Intercession, Praying With Authority*, and *Rise to Your Destiny Woman of God*

We have been blessed by Tommy and Rachel's conferences from those early days when we met in one building until the time they moved into the sprawling complex of buildings—from the kitchen fire to the present waves of thousands of young people being trained for end-time ministry. Tommy and Rachel are indeed among God's generals, and the messages shared in her book are tried and tested instructions from God. This book is a must-read for every Christian.

—PEGGY JOYCE RUTH
Author, *Psalm 91: God's Shield of Protection*

MIRACLE
Moments

RACHEL BURCHFIELD

CHARISMA
HOUSE

Most CHARISMA HOUSE BOOK GROUP products are available at special quantity discounts for bulk purchase for sales promotions, premiums, fund-raising, and educational needs. For details, write Charisma House Book Group, 600 Rinehart Road, Lake Mary, Florida 32746, or telephone (407) 333-0600.

MIRACLE MOMENTS by Rachel Burchfield
Published by Charisma House
Charisma Media/Charisma House Book Group
600 Rinehart Road
Lake Mary, Florida 32746
www.charismahouse.com

Unless otherwise noted, all Scripture quotations are from the New King James Version of the Bible. Copyright © 1979, 1980, 1982 by Thomas Nelson, Inc., publishers. Used by permission.

Scripture quotations marked AMP are from the Amplified Bible. Old Testament copyright © 1965, 1987 by the Zondervan Corporation. The Amplified New Testament copyright © 1954, 1958, 1987 by the Lockman Foundation. Used by permission.

Scripture quotations marked KJV are from the King James Version of the Bible.

Scripture quotations marked NIV are from the Holy Bible, New International Version. Copyright © 1973, 1978, 1984, International Bible Society. Used by permission.

Scripture quotations marked NLT are from the Holy Bible, New Living Translation, copyright © 1996, 2004, 2007. Used by permission of Tyndale House Publishers, Inc., Wheaton, IL 60189. All rights reserved.

Cover design by Justin Evans
Design Director: Bill Johnson

Visit the author's website at http://burchfield.org.

Library of Congress Cataloging-in-Publication Data:
An application to register this book for cataloging has been submitted
to the Library of Congress.
International Standard Book Number: 978-1-62136-304-0
E-book ISBN: 978-1-62136-305-7

Names and details of incidents in this book have been changed,
except those for which permission has been granted. Any similarity
between the names and stories, where changes have been made, in
this book to individuals known to readers is purely coincidental.

While the author has made every effort to provide accurate telephone
numbers and Internet addresses at the time of publication, neither the
publisher nor the author assumes any responsibility for errors or for
changes that occur after publication.

First edition

13 14 15 16 17 — 9 8 7 6 5 4 3 2 1
Printed in the United States of America

To Tommy Burchfield, my best friend and husband of thirty years. You are the love of my life, whom I deeply respect. Thank you for teaching me risky faith, keeping it fun, and enduring my passion for red.

And to my three greatest miracle moments: Andrew, Peter, and Abby, who grew up knowing that the stage was really an altar and now prove their love for Jesus in their commitment to one another.

CONTENTS

ACKNOWLEDGMENTS

BEHIND THIS STORY is an amazing team of friends, each one selflessly fulfilling their invaluable role to build a camp, a Bible school, and later a church to reach the world with God's love. We are forever grateful that they *also* said yes to God's call, and a genuine appreciation goes to:

Our twenty-four-year veterans—my special friend Sophie Gonzales, who exchanged timidity for the purposes of God and evolved into an administrative dynamo; Mike and Kim Wolbrecht, whose unwavering loyalty inspires us all; and Jackie Valenta, who serves behind the scenes yet is seen by Him.

"Me-Emma" K. Smart, whose commitment to crayons and LEGOs filled our home and hearts with joy, and Shayla Garner, a true daughter who empowers us personally.

Predictable Gabe and Heather Munoz, whose music has pointed people to Jesus for seventeen years and who still wear the same size of DC khaki shorts. Mike and Valinda Moilanen, who exchanged a successful career for eternal riches.

My editorial team—Jamie, Megan, Kylee, Rachel, and RJ (All hail, King Caffeine!)

Special honor also belongs to our partner churches and our 120 Covenant Ministry partners whose fervent prayers and faithful offerings have sustained us monthly.

And, last but not least, our former staff who now serve Jesus around the world but left their fingerprints all over our campus—I am forever "the lady who loves you."

PREFACE

SOME HAVE SAID that there never was a day of miracles, but if that is true, the news got to me too late. We never saw a *day* of miracles but a *God* of miracles who is still alive and performing them. Now, you may label me just a simple Texas girl, but I never needed sophisticated data to prove the reality of God's transforming love. The litmus test for me? Watching five hundred thousand campers come to the altar at Discovery Camp over a span of twenty-five years. All kinds too, whether gospel-hardened jocks, seven-year-old first-timers, or pastors ready to resign. Welcome to my world, where it is natural to walk in the supernatural; where all things are possible to those who believe…and work…and learn…and forgive…and dream.

This book is about my husband and me and how—responding to a heavenly call—we left behind a successful ministry in Houston to assume ownership of a small camp. Today our headquarters sits on nearly eleven hundred debt-free acres with accommodations for one thousand guests. This book contains more than our personal story. We hope you will treat it like a manual that invites you to experience a life of miracles.

This manual is quite different from the eye-straining, small-print manuals you may have tossed into your bottom dresser drawer in the past. It's a parenting manual to train you how to fertilize your child's faith. It's a leader's manual filled with visionary data for success and a minister's manual, written to inspire you to anchor on ageless truths while reaching for new anointing. Finally it is also a young adult manual for those of you pondering your three most important choices: 1) your God, 2) your occupation, and 3) your spouse. The answers to Twelve Life Questions, the wisdom of Twelve Life Lessons, and the Twelve Miracle Moments needed to see your dream fulfilled also are sprinkled throughout our miracle story.

Miracle moments can become commonplace, as long as they never become common.

CHAPTER 1

God's Perfect Timing

&v **Life Question:** What takes God so long?

&v **Miracle Moment:** The miracle of trust

&v **Life Lesson:** The good thing didn't happen so the better thing could.

THE SCENE LOOKED LIKE SOMETHING OUT OF A BAD B MOVIE, where banditos routinely trespass across vacant property while sagebrush tumbles by and coyotes howl at the moon. Rumors circulated among the locals that just a few years earlier on Country Camp's property a pack of professional athletes had hosted a "Miss Nude America" pageant. Whether that really happened or sprang from rumormongers' overactive imaginations didn't really matter. Many *believed* the tale. That day, had someone shared the camp's destiny with the locals, they would have shaken their heads in utter disbelief. At first we struggled to grab hold of the vision that this property would become "a headquarters of faith for the youth of the world." The story starts seventy miles to the west in northeast Houston.

"Rachel, I received an interesting phone call today," said my husband, Tommy. "A family who owns a large camp outside of Houston wants to hire me to become their camp director. He mentioned that it has over five hundred acres. The director's house is a two-story brick home shaded by huge oak trees." That didn't raise my eyebrows. We had often hosted camps and retreats for young people,

1

gathering hundreds from the tri-state area of Texas, Louisiana, and Arkansas. In the past several years we had rented Baptist- and Methodist-owned camps, civic centers, and pavilions to accommodate our youth gatherings.

Tommy and I had been married only a year, and he already had a comfortable position as youth director of a megachurch in Houston. So our afternoon journey to the town of Columbus originated primarily from curiosity and a desire to be courteous to the caller. However, upon our arrival, I instantly fell in love with the winding, country road and the ancient oaks lining each side, with the Spanish moss dangling from their limbs taking on the appearance of ethereal, silvery fingers. I sensed something special when we turned onto the large—yet lonely and almost foreboding—Country Camp property. Then I quickly dismissed it as the emotional enticement of escaping the demands of the faithfulness and energy required to maintain a thriving youth group.

Though neglected, the property contained handsome accommodations for two hundred guests. Our minds raced back to the previous year when the administrator of a denominational camp we rented forbid us to clap, dance, or "perform glossalalia." I could still picture it: a scrawny man measuring a mere five feet, five inches tall, pointing a grumpy finger at six feet, three inches tall Tommy as he yelled, "You can have services as late as you'd like, but at ten o'clock tonight the lights and air conditioning will get turned off!"

My husband whispered, "Keep your cool, Sug [Mississippian for "Sugar"]; we'll just ask Jesus to give us our own camp someday." As we toured the large swimming pool and pristine kitchen, I wondered: "Was this our 'someday'?" After all, this was a *large* place, one that would require a *large* vision to operate.

Newlyweds Tommy and Rachel Burchfield

Feeling this represented an opportunity worth praying about, we decided to spend the night, albeit with specific instructions from Tommy: "We'll sleep in separate rooms and wait in prayer for the Lord's direction. In the morning we'll compare notes." Maybe it was the gravity of his instructions or the uncertainty of what lay ahead—including the financial challenges—but I felt troubled in my spirit. I cried out to the Lord in distress, telling Him I desired only His perfect will. I fell asleep hearing Tommy in the master bedroom, loudly praying in the Spirit.

At 6:00 a.m. the Holy Spirit instructed me to turn to Psalm 118:5 for our answer. I had no idea what it said, but I committed to wholeheartedly obey as I fumbled through the pages. Let me be quick to say that opening your Bible and going "eenie-meenie-miney-mo" isn't a wise approach to seeking God's guidance, but this was a "rhema" moment of hearing God's word for me. The Lord had initiated this (in fact, He had guided me this way before), and I didn't treat this nonchalantly. Whatever this verse said, I intended to obey.

After my distress of the previous evening, I held my breath as I read: "I called upon the LORD in distress: the LORD answered me, and set me in a *large* place. The LORD is on my side" (Ps. 118:5, KJV, emphasis added).

I stared at our future in the black and white pages of God's Word. He has a wonderful way of making things plain once you shift your personal desires into neutral. Though I acted as if I were waiting to hear what instructions God had given Tommy, in my mind I was already packing suitcases and decorating the house. When we reunited in the director's kitchen, my heart sank when Tommy said, "This is much too serious of an undertaking to make a decision on our own. Also, we've made a commitment to our pastor. We'll return to Houston and submit this opportunity to him. God will use our pastor to confirm our direction."

It was a long trip home. Along the way I grumbled silently: "Why do we need to get counseling when I've heard from God? What pastor is going to feel Spirit-led to release a competent, well-known youth pastor?" I fussed and fumed the whole drive back to Houston. I felt certain Tommy was making a huge mistake, but our twelve-month marriage had already experienced some bumps. I knew I needed to learn to trust God's direction through my husband.

As if this struggle weren't bad enough, our meeting with the senior pastor drove me deeper into dismay. He laughed at the very idea of moving our well-established youth ministry to a cow pasture community: "Stay here and reach the youth of this city. Don't go chasing every door that swings open."

Bam! It seemed the Country Camp door had slammed shut. But I wasn't about to take this setback like a gracious, submissive newlywed.

DISAPPOINTED AND DISCOURAGED

While Tommy yielded wholeheartedly to our pastor's advice, I kicked, squirmed, and fell into an unshakable depression. I even went as far as traveling to northern Minnesota to spend a week at my parents' house, although I essentially wanted to be alone with God for a week. I sat on the dock overlooking scenic Serpent Lake, but the largemouth bass, walleye, bluegill, and northern pike fish that jumped about its waters couldn't cheer me up. I felt confident that my husband had missed God's plan for our lives. "During sixteen years of serving the Lord," I reasoned, "I've never been out of God's will." I feared the potential consequences of doing so.

With a panic attack threatening to overwhelm me, I thought, "I laid down a successful traveling ministry to marry Tommy. Now I am at the mercy of this man. His decisions now control my life. What if he misses God's voice often? Why would the Lord tell me yes and tell Tommy no concerning this ministry opportunity?"

However, as I sat there on that wooden dock thirteen hundred miles away from my husband, a defining moment in our marriage occurred. Tough as it was, I recognized I had to surrender my know-it-all attitude to Jesus and ask Him to help me trust Tommy's ability to lead us. I had never doubted my love for my husband, and since God had clearly confirmed the *rightness* of our marriage, obviously our disagreement represented a struggle I had to resolve. Though sad, I buried my Country Camp dreams and returned to Texas with a heart to support my husband in whatever ministry he committed us to fulfill. Together we served joyfully in many departments of our church. Still, our zeal to reach young people across the nation kept growing. When we finally resigned five years later, our decision came with the full blessing of our pastor.

Six weeks into our new season of ministry, we received an exciting phone call. Country Camp's owners, who were members of the Assemblies of God, had held things together for five years but now wanted us to pray about taking ownership of the property. Everything I had buried concerning the camp sprang back to life, sparking a new season of prayer and negotiation. All parties involved agreed that this *was* God's plan and perfect timing.

Did Tommy miss God's timing the first time? Not a chance. During that time Tommy established a national reputation. He helped gather five thousand for a youth convention in Houston, learned the logistics of blending ministers, served in the television department, developed a global vision, and learned to live by faith. Me? I learned to trust God in my amazing husband. Five years and two sons later, Tommy's "no" became a "now." Instead of an offer to become the directors, we signed a contract assuming payments for the camp's 553 acres and nine buildings. We became owners instead of employees and CEOs instead of camp directors.

A big miracle in 1989: 553 acres to reach youth

WHAT TAKES GOD SO LONG?

Let me share some basic understanding about God's timing so you can avoid the unneeded emotional drama I endured. God doesn't consult your calendar because His purposes are eternal. Man's calendar says American girls should get married in their twenties and raise children while in their thirties. Maybe so. Maybe no. God knows best.

Secondly, life is not about what you are *doing* but what you are *becoming*. That is why the journey is as important as the destination. When God doesn't jump through our prayer hoops like a trained pony in a circus, we find ourselves forced to humbly accept His plan. Patience and trust are much-needed attributes during these confusing times. Finally, as long as "what" you want trumps the "Who" you want, receiving your "what" would lead you into idolatry. Why? Because God is a jealous God who refuses to compete for your affection. That is why Jesus taught us to "seek first the kingdom of God and His righteousness, and all these things shall be added to you" (Matt. 6:33).

To those who are weary of waiting for God to cooperate with your plans, make certain that the Lord Jesus comes first in your life. I am confident that as you pursue the "Who" wholeheartedly, your "what" will either arrive or that desire will drift away.

I learned so much from this divine delay of my dreams. That experience and subsequent study of the Scriptures showed me how He will implement perfect plans if only we will let Him and avoid forcing the issue. Likewise, on your journey with God you can glean several life principles about His timing from the Israelites' trip from Egypt to the Promised Land. I can see five reasons God delayed their trip.

Protection

God didn't guide the children of Israel down the shortest route. He gave them a divine detour so they wouldn't change their minds and return to Egypt when they saw war (Exod. 13:17).

A critical attitude

When Miriam criticized her younger brother's choice for a wife, God struck her with leprosy and detained two million people for seven days (Num. 12:10).

To test their hearts

God will test your heart so He can expose anything detrimental and thereby prevent emotional, physical, or spiritual destruction. If you obey, He will always do you good in the end (Deut. 8:16).

Doubt

The Israelites could have trekked to their Promised Land in two and a half weeks, yet they *"limited the Holy One"* (v. 41, emphasis added) and wandered for forty years (Ps. 78:19, 41).

A bigger picture

Why did God require them to possess their Promised Land *"little by little"*? He was protecting them from wild animals! (See Deuteronomy 7:22.) Is it possible God knows something you don't? While you may know what you want, He knows what you need. Trust Him.

TWO TYPES OF WAITING

Have you ever taken a loved one to the hospital for surgery? For those who haven't, let me describe it. After you give the patient's hand a squeeze and kiss his head, orderlies roll his stretcher down the hallway while directing you to the waiting room. *Ugh.* Even that name annoys me. In the waiting room time stands still. This cleverly decorated cage attempts to soften the reality that your schedule and future are at someone else's mercy. As you look around, you observe a room crowded with sleeping captives, their legs pretzeled into small chairs. Yep, you're gonna miss lunch, and it ain't gonna be any fun.

Is this a picture of waiting on the Lord? No, it is a miserable misconception. Biblical waiting is action-packed. The Hebrew word rendered "wait upon" is *qavah*, which denotes to wait in the sense of expecting, to put our hope or confidence in Him. It implies intentionality, not inactivity. This word is a verb and carries the connotation of strenuous endeavors to secure an object or fulfill one's needs. Therefore, to wait upon the Lord is to fulfill His every need. What could our God, the Creator of the universe, possibly need from you? Your passionate praise, an undivided heart, and total trust.

You don't wait on the Lord as if you would wait in a long line or for an overdue bus. A better example is a bride eagerly awaiting her wedding. She is contacting people to assist her while organizing a plethora of details. There are invitations to order, bridesmaids' dresses to select, and the perfect wedding cake to design. If you have personally experienced the wedding whirlwind, you can testify that twiddling your thumbs didn't appear on the schedule.

For male readers who struggle to grasp the wedding scenario, consider a waiter at a fine restaurant. His objective is to fulfill the needs of his guests. He isn't twiddling his thumbs either. With both examples a reward occurs at the end of the wait: a husband or a generous gratuity. Likewise, waiting on the Lord also brings rewards: "Wait on the Lord; be of good courage, and He shall strengthen your heart; wait, I say, on the LORD!" (Ps. 27:14).

LIFE IS NOT ALWAYS PRETTY

You can liken learning to trust in God's timing to working a jigsaw puzzle. There you sit, trying to make sense of the hundreds (even thousands) of tiny pieces scattered around the table. Life sometimes feels that way, with all the "happys" and "sads" scrambled around in one box. *Where do you start?* As a puzzle master I'll tell you: with the four corner pieces. To make your life-puzzle a pretty picture, I suggest these four cornerstones will help you trust God's timing.

CORNER #1: God is all-loving.

While dealing with what seems to be utter silence, remember the first cornerstone of your life-puzzle is God's love. He takes no delight in watching you go through your day lonely or fearful, looking over your shoulder and waiting for a heavenly hammer to fall. No. A thousand times no! God is a Father. Do you know any father who takes pleasure in his son's sorrow or sickness? He is your Father and won't withhold anything good from you. He loves you as much as Jesus: "He that spared not his own Son...how shall he not with him also freely give us all things?" (Rom. 8:32, KJV). Stop reading this instant and say this out loud: "Heavenly Father, help me to receive Your love right now."

CORNER #2: God is all-knowing.

God's omniscience confuses our finite minds. Psalm 139:2–3 reveals the touching truth that God knows "my sitting down and my rising up; You understand my thought afar off. You comprehend my path and my lying down, and are acquainted with all my ways." The lyrics to the familiar children's song say, "Jesus loves me, this I know...,"[1] but it could also be sung, "Jesus knows me, this I love." God knows you and still chose you. He knows the good and bad choices of your past and everything that people will do to you in the future. He knows all the parts of your life—the fair and the unfair, the just and unjust, positive and negative. In His infinite foreknowledge this magnificent God sees every second of your life.

CORNER #3: God is all-powerful.

While waiting for God's perfect timing, many believers fall into the trap of blaming the devil for the delay. They conclude that it's the devil's fault that their dreams have not come true.

Ever hear the old joke about the Christian walking home from church when he notices the devil sitting on the curb? His face buried in his hands, Satan is sobbing uncontrollably. Distraught by the devil's anguish, the kindhearted believer sits down on the curb and compassionately says, "Tell me what is so terribly wrong that you are sobbing this uncontrollably?" Barely lifting his head, the devil mutters, "It's those Christians! They blame me for everything."

Friends, God is all-powerful and exceedingly greater than the devil. According to 2 Chronicles 16:9 God will "show Himself strong on behalf of those whose heart is loyal to Him." Nothing is too difficult for God. He can bring you a fiancé from an underground church in China, translate him to Los Angeles, and put him on a Greyhound bus destined for your front door.

CORNER #4: God is faithful.

The fourth corner that will keep you sane while waiting on His perfect timing is remembering God's faithfulness. He is dependable and reliable. Remembering this will help you maintain the proper perspective on life. You can choose one of two outlooks: 1) God in *your* story or 2) you in *God's* story. The first is idolatry and the other is truth. Here is a truth author Joy Dawson has shared and one that will help you to avoid making demands on the Lord: It's not about you. It's not about making your life perfect but making His name known. The reason you absolutely must know this is because God is only faithful to His Word, not your every whim.

There is a bigger picture, and you have been invited to share in its fulfillment. Once you get this, your priorities will shift. You will stop fretting about unfulfilled personal needs. When you want what God wants more than what you want, life is wonderful. This is where the famous phrase from the Lord's Prayer, "Thy will be done" (Matt. 6:10, KJV) applies, revealing itself as a life of daily surrender to His plan. It is also where "the desire of the righteous will be granted" (Prov. 10:24) applies. If you are battling disappointment, put God first in your life. You can trust Him with those buried hopes and dreams. He will be faithful to fulfill His Word in you.

Remember, you have a beautiful promise waiting for you. As

Ecclesiastes 3:11 promises: "He has made everything beautiful in its time." As you continually focus on a Father God who is all-loving, all-knowing, all-powerful, and faithful, you can expect a perfect peace to replace your impatience and anxieties. God's ways are perfect, and so is His timing.

A Delay Is Not a Denial

When famed evangelist George Müller was in his early twenties, he made several unsuccessful attempts to fulfill this calling. Although he sensed God's call in his heart, nothing seemed to quite work out. When he didn't see the fulfillment of this dream, Müller gave up. When he was sixty-seven years of age, the gifts and callings of God materialized, and for the next twenty years Müller earned a reputation as one of the nineteenth century's foremost Christian statesmen, traveling thousands of miles and speaking at multiple mission outreaches.[2]

Several Bible characters experienced the agony of waiting. After spending a century building the ark, Noah spent more than a year after the flood waiting for the waters to recede. (And you thought you had patience!) Joseph spent at least three years in prison waiting for God's perfect timing of his release. Samuel anointed David for God's service as a youth of seventeen, but David faced a twenty-year wait to become king of Israel. Abraham waited twenty-five years for his promised child. Waiting on God requires you to trust in His character and His goodness, and it is never, ever a waste of time.

The Ways of an Eagle

"But those who wait on the Lord shall renew their strength; they shall mount up with wings like eagles, they shall run and not be weary, they shall walk and not faint" (Isa. 40:31). This is just one of more than twenty vivid examples of an eagle in the Bible, each one lending insight to the valuable benefits of waiting on the Lord.

The eagle's eyes, mounting up, soaring techniques, and renewal processes all contain significance when it comes to learning to actively wait on God.

An eagle has such keen eyes that one can see a rabbit moving from a mile away. From an altitude of 984 feet, it can spot prey over 3 square miles. Once an eagle's eyes have locked onto its helpless victim, researchers have clocked its devouring dive at up to 150 miles per hour. What an inspirational challenge for us to develop our eyes on pleasing God! A leading benefit of waiting on the Lord is how it refocuses our priorities. We need to be certain that His plan and purpose for our lives are preeminent; nothing can accomplish that as quickly as a few moments in His presence. Composer Helen Lemmel put it beautifully in her legendary 1922 hymn "Turn Your Eyes Upon Jesus":

> Turn your eyes upon Jesus
> Look full in His wonderful face,
> And the things of earth will grow strangely dim,
> In the light of His wonderful grace.[3]

An eagle also possesses an amazing ability to predict the coming of a storm. As turbulent weather moves closer, an internal instinct inspires this majestic creature to fly upward, sometimes to an altitude of ten thousand feet—the "mounting up" Isaiah describes. Just think of it. While the rest of nature falls victim to the storm's destructive forces, the eagle misses its fury altogether. Did you know that trusting in God's perfect timing can prevent many storms in your life?

Once the eagle reaches a safe altitude, he spreads those mighty wings and soars. Soaring, also known as gliding, occurs as the bird catches thermal wind currents, causing it to conserve energy and travel effortlessly at speeds of up to fifty miles per hour.[4] Just as the eagle finds great pleasure and draws strength from soaring, when you place your total trust in God, you will discover His strength carrying you through life.

The eagle's daily cleansing habits can also teach us much about keeping our hearts pure. The average wingspan of a female bald eagle measures a magnificent seven-plus feet. The tips' jagged feathers catch the winds at a certain angle, causing it to rise high and dive quickly in seconds. The eagle gives the greatest of care to each individual feather through a "steam cleaning" process known as preening. To refresh, the bird brings each feather through its mouth, exhaling or breathing on it. A gland in its mouth secretes an oily substance—which enables it to soar during storms or fly into water without getting bogged down (waterproofing at its best). It takes an hour each day to cleanse the twelve hundred feathers on each wing, and more for larger birds. Should we not also take time to ask the Holy Spirit to help keep our hearts clean and avoid getting bogged down with attitudes contrary to His ways?

Eagles can teach us much about waiting as well. If you are grappling with disappointment and feel too weary to continue waiting, consider the plight of an older eagle that endures a much-needed renewal during its forty-year life span. As they age, eagles' flight speed lessens, with duller talons making it difficult to grab prey too. Its worn feathers whistle as it dives for food, warning prey of its advance. With weaker wings it spends more time walking in the valley. Its nostrils fill up with calcium. It cannot breathe sufficiently to vigorously preen its feathers.

Recognizing that it needs renewal, an aging eagle washes its feathers in a nearby stream or river. It seeks a crevice in a high cliff where it can pluck out old, useless feathers. Finally the tired bird finds itself vulnerable to predators. Scratching its talons until they are nubs, it flies directly into the rock until its beak breaks off. When it is fresh, clean, and naked, it lies "spread eagle" on the rock, getting as close to the sun as possible. Unable to feed itself, it must depend on older eagles dropping it fresh meat until it can regain the strength to feed itself. However, this weary eagle receives new life. Its feathers begin to grow back, and its talons and beak regain sharpness. The once-droopy wings are ready to soar as its hunger arouses it to fly and storms inspire it to once again soar.[5]

What a powerful picture this portrays for us, an apt reminder to diligently wait on the Lord. The same Creator who nudges the eagle to rise above a storm will nudge His children to do the same. Obeying the gentle promptings of the Holy Spirit will keep our eyes focused on eternal approval, keep our hearts cleansed daily, and create a dependence on Him. Worshipping and waiting on the Son will cause us to soar.

FLY, EAGLE, FLY

You might be tempted to whine while you wait for God's perfect timing, but here's a story I hope will inspire you to be a soaring eagle instead of a complaining chicken. It involves a large, awkward egg that fell from the nest into a chicken yard. Out emerged the oddest-looking chicken the others had ever seen. Looking at his newfound friends, the new bird said, "Where am I? Who am I?"

The chickens replied, "You're a chicken, and you're with us in the barnyard."

"What do chickens do?" he asked.

"Chickens peck," they replied.

So his life went. Peck. Peck. Peck. Days, weeks, and month passed. Peck. Peck. Peck.

"Sure seems boring," he said one day. "I think that I was born to do something besides pecking." Then, after looking skyward, he exclaimed, "Oh, my! Look at that bird soaring. That's what I want to do."

A gale of laughter filled the barnyard. One chicken explained, "You can't do that. That's an eagle, and only eagles can soar that high.

You are a chicken. All you get to do is peck, peck, peck." After a while the little bird got tired of pecking, so he started to flap his wings. Though he only rose a few inches, a soft voice within prodded him on: "You were born to fly. Leave these chickens behind you. You were born to fly."

Much to the scorn of the chickens, the strange little bird realized he was really an eagle, and up, up, up he flew, soaring as all eagles do. When God seems to be taking too long, you can choose to become as this little eagle. Don't spend your days thinking as a chicken as you peck, peck, peck: "God doesn't love me." Peck. Peck. Peck. "I don't deserve to get blessed." Peck. Peck. Peck. "God has forgotten me."

Refuse to meditate on such chicken thoughts. Listen to these internal whispers, "You were born to fly. Trust Me. Don't look at your problem. Rise up now and flap those wings of worship." Soon you will be gazing in the face of the Son, and nothing you long for will matter.

THE MIRACLE OF TRUST

The greatest revelation that I've ever received is that God is smarter than I am.

—John Osteen[6]

Teach us, O Lord, the disciplines of patience, for to wait is often harder than to work.

—Peter Marshall[7]

A delay is not always a denial.

—Author unknown

I realized that the deepest spiritual lessons are not learned by His letting us have our way in the end, but by His making us wait, bearing with us in love and patience until we are able to honestly to pray what He taught His disciples to pray: Thy will be done.

—Elisabeth Elliot[8]

CHAPTER 2

The Big Move

&❧ **Life Question:** How do miracle moments begin?

&❧ **Miracle Moment:** The miracle of faith

&❧ **Life Lesson:** God's voice always agrees with God's Word.

WHAT DOES IT MEAN TO LIVE BY FAITH? AND WHY DOES IT please God so greatly? Living by faith is when you know the next "what" on your eternal calendar but not the "how," "when," or "where." It is a great adventure that connects you to an invisible realm of provision. Do you remember when the disciples were rowing the boat and Jesus came to them, walking on the water?

When the invitation came, only Peter climbed out of the boat. Wanting to be in Christ's presence, he left eleven "experts" in the boat, committed to their routine of rowing and explaining why it wouldn't work. I would caution here: Be steadfast in your routines until Jesus invites you to do otherwise. But if you want to please God and walk by faith and not by sight, sooner or later you will have to get out of the boat.

That is what happened to us. After ten years of full-time ministry in the Houston area, God spoke to us about pursuing a new type of ministry for young people. We had attempted this five years earlier, but you may remember from chapter 1 that our pastor didn't agree with the idea. Another few years passed, and just before we resigned, our beloved pastor had unexpected heart surgery. Tommy felt that he needed us then more than ever. So for a second time we postponed our plans.

THE BIG GOOD-BYE

Finally in October of 1988, with our pastor's full and public blessing, we bid good-bye to our church family, a thriving youth group, and the financial security of a salary. We ministered at several youth conventions as we waited on God for the "how, where, and when." For several weeks I heard in my Spirit, "Say good-bye and say hello." But what did that mean?

That fall my father lay near death in St. Joseph's Hospital, still not born again. For twenty years I had prayed for his salvation and claimed his soul for Jesus. Less than two months after we left our church, the Spirit of God jolted me awake at 6:06 a.m. (Whether human or divine, I seem to remember all the times of early-morning wake-up calls.) I could hear Him as if He had placed a megaphone in my ear: "Today is your father's day of salvation. Go now and demand of him his soul."

"Now?" I questioned.

It didn't seem like the most practical time to drive thirty miles in the dark. Not only was I seven months pregnant, but Daddy was also unconscious. Nevertheless I listened. In the waiting room sat Mom, quite surprised to see me.

"Rachel! Why are you here so early?" she asked.

"Mama, Jesus has sent me to pray a salvation prayer with Daddy. Today is his day for salvation," I said with a smile.

"Oh, honey, he's been unconscious for most of the night. Don't be disappointed if..."

In my spirit I didn't have time to hear her finish. Quietly I entered the hospital room. There sat my one-of-a-kind daddy, totally alert and practically sitting up in bed.

"Cutie pie! Why are you here so early?" said my good-natured (but church-hardened) father.

"Daddy, I've come to get you ready for eternity."

Though tender and respectful, I was blunt. I gave him no choice in the matter. I told him it was time. After years of prayer and effort, he willingly repeated a salvation prayer (timing is everything). Sixty seconds after his "amen," a loud knock sounded at the door, and in rolled a stretcher pushed by two white-suited men. "Mr. Cook?" said one. "We've come to take you to X-ray." They were stunned that he was conscious and alert.

On the drive home I shouted out loud, "Ha ha on you, Satan! You lost a soul today."

Then, in a flash, as I glanced through the drizzly, cold rain, I saw a car headed directly for my front left hood. As I heard the words "fiery dart," I knew that the inevitable collision represented revenge for Dad's salvation and an effort to thwart the destiny of our second son. Grabbing for my pregnant belly, I screamed on his behalf, "I claim life!"

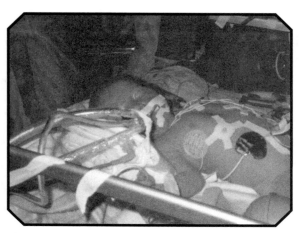

Baby Peter in ICU

GOOD-BYE AND HELLO

I gave birth to Peter Nicholas prematurely. Of all places the ambulance transported us to St. Joseph's intensive care unit. There Tommy and I fought for life—for our baby on the first floor and Daddy on the second. Meanwhile Tommy and I had no salary or church family for support, but we had faith in God. We had deliberately broken ranks with well-meaning friends and relatives who questioned our decision to walk by faith. Granted, fear and genuine concern fueled most of the harsh comments directed at us. I could understand: No job. No plans. New baby.

Six weeks later Tommy and I ministered at Daddy's funeral, listening to our tiny son's faint whimpers from the back row. As I kissed Daddy's earthly shell, I said good-bye to the natural world. Then I hugged our miracle baby and said hello to our new supernatural life. Thus began our preparation for the next twenty-five years of walking by faith. It only sounds easy looking back. You may face the same difficult choice and need to break ranks with negative influences, those well-meaning people who don't understand a walk of faith. Perhaps now is the season for you to "trust in the LORD with all your heart, and lean not on your own understanding" (Prov. 3:5). Because I did, my father is in heaven. Today Peter is a strong, lanky youth pastor who preaches to thousands.

PROGRESSIVE FAITH

The ways of God concerning His guidance have always intrigued me. While being an eternal God, He still kindly leads us step by step. We should be grateful that He doesn't show us His ten-year plan. Although usually clear on the "what," He seems vague on the "how," "where," and "when" categories. God gave us a clear mandate on the what: to reach youth and train church workers. Yet the details were pretty fuzzy. If you feel the same way, could it be possible that while you are waiting on God, the reality is that He is waiting on you?

Does He care how we accomplish the task? If you send a friend to the store for bread, do you care which route he follows? Perhaps God is not quite as concerned about the "how," "when," and "where" as much as the "what."

Progressive faith is divine information released in increments, which demonstrates God's pattern of leading us little by little, just as God didn't lead the Israelites on the shortest route to Mount Sinai so they could avoid a collision with intimidating heathen tribes. He nurtured a progressive development of David's confidence, starting with killing a lion and a bear, which led to his climatic confrontation with Goliath. Psalm 37:23 says, "The *steps* of a good man are ordered by the LORD," not our bounding leaps. I liken God's guidance to a game of checkers. After He whispers (or thunders) a hint, it is your move. Don't expect another e-mail from eternity until you have completed the previous one.

Small beginnings, big dreams for Discovery Camp

FINALLY!

Once we knew God's timing had arrived, we became like a pregnant woman consumed with the impending birth. We constantly compared notes about reaching young people and the best ways to gather and train church workers. Every meal out evolved into our dream lists based on Habakkuk 2:3, which talks of waiting on God's vision. The diagrams and outlines scribbled on paper napkins became souvenirs of destiny.

Because Tommy is excruciatingly responsible with our finances, he agonized over the timing of our move. However, as I previously noted, sooner or later you have to get out of the boat. Doing so will never make sense to experts who remain in the boat. Nor will your well-meaning, worried friends and relatives affirm your decision. When someone asks you if people will support your step of faith, smile big and say, "S.W.S.W.S.W." That is my acronym for "Some Will; Some Won't; So What?" While being teachable is important, if you have heard from God on a matter (and have a record of getting it right), get out of the boat. Walk on water with Jesus.

On May 6, 1989, Tommy and I packed our dreams, belongings, and two young sons into a yellow Ryder truck. We left behind all the successes and security connected to our well-established church position and reputation. Most of our mentors thought we were making a huge mistake. After all, several organizations with more financial backing and experience had attempted to make a go of this camp before hitting a dead end. Fortunately we didn't have enough sense to be scared. Why? We knew that God always rewards faith. With our inner checklist complete, it was time to move.

Our experience showed me that many times God's leading will make no sense to our natural reasoning. You might be in that situation where you believe the Lord is leading you to do something contrary to human wisdom. First you must answer this big question: Are you positive that you are hearing God's voice? If so, you will be abundantly blessed. If not, you will face abundant disillusionment. There are several things you can do to assure you are walking in faith instead of presumption. The most important is recognizing that His voice and His Word always agree. As an example, God will

never tell you to use your company's credit card for personal pleasures because His Word tells us not to steal. (It may be common,
but it's still stealing!)

Presumptuous faith occurs when people haven't learned how to
discern the source of the voice speaking to them. Once you know the
Word of God, it won't represent rocket science. For new believers let
me expose some obvious mistakes. Tommy and I have heard some
goofy things over the years that were supposedly "from the Lord."
To name several:

+ God's voice will never tell you to quit attending
  church since His Word instructs us to "not [forsake]
  the assembling of ourselves together" (Heb. 10:25).

+ God's voice will never tell you to be emotionally or
  sexually involved with anyone other than your spouse.

+ God's voice will never tell you to quit paying your bills,
  even if the money is going to a reputable charity.

+ God's voice will never tell you to get counseling from
  a friend whose life is in more of a mess than yours.

+ God's voice will never contradict God's Word. Never.
  That would be as foolish as you telling your son to eat
  the last burger while you throw it into the trash.

Back in the mid-1990s we learned that two young students from
our Texas Bible Institute (TBI) were sleeping together in a hotel.
The young man told me sincerely, "Ms. Rachel, it was the Lord's
idea." Not only did his tone of his voice reflect confusion, his explanation was equally bizarre: "I was sexually active before I gave my
life to Jesus, so I know how important it is to be sexually compat-
ible. I really do love her and plan to marry her someday. We even got

down on our knees next to that hotel bed and prayed, 'Lord, if You want us to get married, then let our time together be extra special.'"

Bless their hearts. As veterans in young ministry, we don't get duped too often. Yet I believe this young man felt sure that this "sex-periment" was God's idea. As for the girl, she had been raised in church and knew better but yielded to raging hormones. I quietly explained to them that the voice of God would never contradict the Word of God. Since God's Word forbids premarital sex, His voice would never lead them into sin. They repented and finished the year at TBI while learning the correct way to discern God's voice.

I have created an "I've Heard From God" checklist that can help confirm whether you really heard something from Him or you ate too much pizza with anchovies before falling asleep.

My "I've Heard From God" Checklist

_____ **Does this agree with Scripture?**

God's voice never contradicts His Word. A ready example is marrying an unbeliever on the theory you can change him or simply because she is so attractive. God would never tell you to do this. His Word clearly says, "Do not be unequally yoked together with unbelievers" (2 Cor. 6:14).

_____ **Do you have an inner witness?**

Romans 8:16 says that all believers have an inward witness. I call it "your knower." In your deepest being His children recognize the things of God. You will know that you know that you know.

_____ **Are you accountable to your pastor? Teachable?**

Pastors should not act as all-knowing masters, but if you face a major decision, it is wise to allow this person or someone with spiritual maturity to help guide you. God anoints pastors to guide and guard His people.

_____ **Do you have peace in your spirit?**

You can have perfect peace in your spirit while your mind is screaming crazy thoughts. To affirm what I mentioned earlier in this chapter: "Trust in the LORD with all your heart, and lean not on your own understanding" (Prov. 3:5).

_____ **Would Jesus do this?**

When in doubt, consider Christ's example. It also helps to contemplate a spiritual mentor. Can you imagine that person doing what you feel led to do?

_____ **Would a loving father do this?**

God is a loving Father, and His voice will reflect that. I would question any demanding voice that separates families (emotionally) or is self-destructive.

_____ **Have you received a confirmation?**

A confirmation is when God says the same exact thing more than once in a different way. (See Matthew 18:16.) If your decision is important or will affect many people, ask Him to confirm His voice and He will, perhaps through a person, a scripture, or an unusual circumstance.

_____ **Are you willing to wait for God's timing?**

You can do the right thing at the wrong time and really struggle. People tend to jump too soon, but God's timing is perfect.

FAITH THAT SEEMS FOOLISH

Sometimes God requires a seemingly foolish action before your miracle will occur. This is where the idea that "there's a miracle on the other side of your obedience" applies. Feeling foolish is just part of the process, but "he who comes to God must believe that He is, and that He is a rewarder of those who diligently seek Him" (Heb. 11:6).

Who am I?

"My barren wife and I followed an invisible voice a thousand miles from the comforts of home, and I became the father of many nations when I was ninety-nine years old" (Answer: Abraham).

"When enemy armies were closing in on us, I obeyed God's unusual military strategy and put the praisers in front of the soldiers" (Answer: Jehoshaphat).

"My four friends carried me on a stretcher and lowered my paralyzed body through the roof so that Jesus could heal me" (Unknown, but healed).

"I broke rank with my other blind friends who told me to shut up, but Jesus honored my faith and I was healed." (Answer: Bartimaeus).

"We resisted the temptation to be ordinary and, against all odds, built a headquarters of faith for the youth of the world" (Answer: Tommy and Rachel Burchfield).

Here are five more examples from the Scriptures that will prove, in the walk of faith, that His voice must trump your natural reasoning. If you sincerely believe it's the voice of the Lord (and it's not illegal, immoral, or fattening), do it!

The boss with a knife

Despite his wife's advanced age and barren status, Abram received a promise of posterity. Believing God, he responded in faith. When a young servant asked his supervisor, "What's this important meeting about?" the man replied, "Something about a vision the boss man had the other night." Then Abram arrived with a knife and an announcement: "The God of the stars has promised me thousands of descendants and told me to circumcise all of you immediately. You will each come into my tent, lift your robe for this procedure, and take off work for three days. Sorry, guys, no sex for two weeks, but when you do feel better, your seed will be blessed by the Most High." Can you imagine the strange looks among his male staff members? (See Genesis 17.)

A water fountain in the rock

Although he led the Hebrew people to freedom, that didn't prevent Moses from facing 2.5 million thirsty murmurers in the desert.[1] "Lord, what do I do?" he asked. "Moses, strike that rock with your rod and water will gush out," God replied. Sounds pretty foolish, don't you think? (See Exodus 17:1–7.)

Big God tests big shot

Naaman's only hope of healing from leprosy: a six-hundred-fifty-mile trek to meet the prophet Elisha.[2] He almost lost his miracle by deeming the prophet's directions a humiliating insult. Dip in the Jordan River seven times? How beneath the dignity of a prestigious military leader. Fortunately a servant advised he listen. When Naaman responded in faith, his skin turned as new as a babe's. (See 2 Kings 5:1–19).

Gold coin in fish's mouth

I would be remiss to skip Jesus's casual instruction to Peter concerning their taxes. To paraphrase Matthew 17:27: "Relax, Peter. Go fishing and you'll find a gold coin in the mouth of the first fish. Use that to pay our taxes." Keep in mind that Peter spent many of his earlier years as a fisherman. How foolish he must have felt! Yet he trusted in Jesus's word. Peter fulfilled his part in the natural, and Jesus fulfilled His part in the supernatural.

Job (in)security?

If your supervisor instructed you to spread toothpaste on your employer's sandwich instead of mayonnaise, would you obey? That is how foolish Jesus's instructions appeared to the servants at the wedding in Cana (John 2:1–11). Instead of wine, take dirty water used for washing hands to the governor? However, faith is simple when you do what Jesus says. As my husband often preaches: "Somewhere from the dip to the sip, Jesus honored that servant's faith, and dirty water became wine."

God rewards faith, so let me repeat: sooner or later you have to get out of the boat. The phrase "according to your faith" gives you a scriptural permission slip to ask Him for big things and expect unexplainable miracles. Your miracle lies on the other side of obedience.

Five Facts About Faith

Faith is agreeing with God and acting on His Word. Although many say they agree with God about an issue, they are just giving mental assent. Assent admires but doesn't act. Others act out a certain way, but it is only behavior modification. They confess a certain scripture, but do they *believe?* Faith is *agreeing* with God and *acting* on His Word. Here are five facts that describe real Bible faith.

Fact #1: Faith is a law.

Motorists everywhere understand that if a streetlight turns red, they must stop. You don't even need to feel a peace in your spirit or goose bumps on your arms. If you obey the law, the police will honor you. If you don't, you will suffer the consequences. The definition of a law is a binding rule of conduct or action, one formally recognized as binding. It is enforced by a controlling authority. The government licenses you to use their roads and will enforce that right—as long as you obey their laws. Romans 3:27 says that faith is a law that entitles you to all of the promises of God. Just as a policeman would enforce the red light law, your Father God enforces His laws of faith.

Fact #2: Faith is a measure.

The typical kitchen contains many different-sized measuring utensils. Yours likely has your favorite scratched-up, three-quart pan that Grandma used, plus a new set of shiny measuring scoops, ranging from one-fourth cup to one cup. I like to stack my little scoopers inside the next larger size. Likewise, when you accepted

Christ, you received a measure or capacity of faith. As you act on God's Word, your one-fourth scoop of faith enlarges to a half scoop.

This is why Jesus said, "According to your faith let it be to you" (Matt. 9:29). Jesus rebuked the disciples for having no faith in the storm and little faith concerning provision, but He marveled at the Roman centurion's great faith. These are different measures of faith. Believing enlarges yours. And faith pleases God. As Hebrews 11:6 says, "But without faith it is impossible to please Him, for he who comes to God must believe that He is, and that He is a rewarder of those who diligently seek Him."

FACT #3: Faith is a muscle.

Imagine a pair of thirty-year-old men smiling at you. One is a tanned bodybuilder, the other looks like a bleached flagpole. One bench-presses five hundred pounds while the other would struggle with the barbell alone. While both have more than six hundred muscles, the difference is the bodybuilder developed his. Many people don't realize that they can develop their faith in the same way a bodybuilder develops his muscles.

FACT #4: Faith is a servant.

Luke contains an interesting story about the role of a servant. Jesus asked His disciples what master—after his servant had plowed a field—would invite him to sit down and eat instead of telling him to prepare the master's supper first? He asked: "Does he thank that servant because he did the things that were commanded him? I think not. So likewise you, when you have done all those things which you are commanded, say, 'We are unprofitable servants. We have done what was our duty to do'" (Luke 17:9–10).

The point is that the master commands the servant. John 1:1 tells us that Jesus, our Master, is the Word. When you speak the Word, your "servant" goes to work to accomplish its assignment. To put it another way, the Word spoke to people, trees, storms, and death, commanding them to obey His voice. When you speak faith-filled words, it is the same as when Jesus spoke them. This is why "with God all things are possible" (Matt. 19:26).

FACT #5: Faith is a seed.

The story of the seed and the sower is recorded in all three Synoptic Gospels—Matthew 13, Mark 4, and Luke 8. Repetition alone implies that this parable contains a significant message. The seed is the Word released from our mouths. Isaiah promises that God's Word, described as seed to the sower, will never return empty or be useless. The seed has dominion over the soil and makes it bud. When you speak God's Word, you are planting seeds of salvation and abundant life. Just as a gardener waters his plants, speaking and praying God's Word causes His goodness to grow in your life and your loved ones' lives.

AGGRESSIVE FAITH

Biblically based faith is by nature aggressive. It is a divine force that operates like a bulldozer, pushing aside anything that gets in its way. As Tommy, me, and our staff applied these foundations of faith diligently, we watched a cow pasture become a "headquarters of faith for the youth of the world." What do you dream of accomplishing with the Lord? All things are possible to those who believe. There are at least seven people who received their miracle from Jesus as a result of their aggressive faith:

Real Person / Real Problem	Scripture Reference	Jesus Said
Woman with a twelve-year hemorrhage	Matt. 9:22; Mark 5:34; Luke 8:48	"Your faith has made you well."
Two blind men	Matt. 9:29	"According to your faith let it be to you."

Real Person / Real Problem	Scripture Reference	Jesus Said
Unchurched mom with a demon-possessed daughter	Matt. 15:28	"O woman, great is your faith! Let it be to you as you desire."
Blind Bartimaeus	Mark 10:52; Luke 18:42	"Your faith has made you well."
Sinful woman who crashed Simon's dinner party	Luke 7:50	"Your faith has saved you. Go in peace."
Ten lepers	Luke 17:19	"Arise, go your way. Your faith has made you well."
Roman centurion with paralyzed employee	Matt. 8:13	"Go your way; and as you have believed, so let it be done for you."

The common denominators among these miracle recipients: they aggressively pursued Jesus, resisted human opinion, ignored all opposition, broke religious and cultural laws, and became believers, not beggars. Did Jesus heal everyone? No, but He healed everyone who asked Him for a miracle. Their faith in a loving, living Jesus brought them a solution. Read and meditate on their stories several times while allowing faith to rise up in you. Jesus can help you or anyone else. Hebrews 13:8 assures: "Jesus Christ is the same yesterday, today and forever."

BULLDOG FAITH

What is the difference between a woman of faith and a bulldog? Lipstick. Even though I had no mentors, I learned the laws of faith as a teen. The Holy Spirit would often train me as I visited churches, whispering things such as, "Pay particular attention to how he prays. He whines like a beggar; I don't reward beggars. I reward believers." I gleaned another lesson during a summer visit to my grandparents' lake in northern Minnesota. Friends there and I liked to swing on a tree rope. As kids often do, we got the crazy idea to train the neighbor's bulldog to grip that rope with his teeth. Indeed, Wilbur never let go. Finally when we ran into the house for watermelon, the Holy Spirit spoke: "Look at Wilbur. That's a picture of faith. When I give you promises, no matter how big, don't let go." Later I noticed the dog still dangling in mid-air from the now-still rope. We taught Wilbur how to grab the knot but not how to let go. What a picture of aggressive faith!

Dr. Alamo Cactus Tumbleweed (Peter) explains how big God is.

Walking by faith requires a corresponding action to Christ's words. Note that Paul didn't instruct us to "sit by faith" but to "walk by faith" (2 Cor. 5:7). Highlight the many times that Jesus required some type of action from those seeking a miracle. When dealing with a leper needing healing, He said, "Arise, go your way. Your faith has made you well" (Luke 17:19), which confirmed that faith is not passive. Now faith doesn't follow formulaic steps or simple 1-2-3s. It isn't that you can push a button, pull a lever, and out comes the answer. Real faith is responding to Jesus, the living Word—His ideas, promptings, suggestions, and promises. You must receive the Miracle Worker.

DARE TO BELIEVE

One sunny afternoon a tourist watched a fisherman on the pier of a picturesque lake. Every time he caught a fish, the fisherman pulled out a tape measure before tossing some back in the lake. Surprisingly the fisherman rejected the large fish while placing the little ones in a bucket. Finally the curious tourist asked, "Why do you throw back the big fish?" With a demeaning expression the man replied, "Because my skillet is only six inches wide."

Did you realize that God might be giving you some big ideas? Don't toss them back just because your faith is still small. Exercise it. Grow in faith. Exchange small ideas for God's big ones. If your dreams don't scare you, you are probably dreaming too small. In fact, if you are pursuing something you can achieve through human talent and ability, I suggest buying a twelve-inch skillet. You will see a big catch of faith when there is no way human way your dreams can come true and you recognize that only God can fulfill them. Faith is agreeing with God and acting on His Word. Faith pleases God and releases Him to work on your behalf. Happy fishing!

THE MIRACLE OF FAITH

I am what God says I am. I have what God says I have. I can do what God says I can do.

—E. W. Kenyon[3]

Faith is . . . a living, daring confidence in God's grace, so sure and certain that a man could stake his life on it a thousand times.

—Martin Luther[4]

The way to see by faith, is to shut the Eye of Reason.

—Benjamin Franklin[5]

Faith is to believe what we do not see; and the reward of this faith is to see what we believe.

—Saint Augustine[6]

Our confession (of faith) builds the road over which faith hauls its mighty cargo.

—E. W. Kenyon[7]

Most people say what they have, when God said we can have what we say.

—Charles Capps[8]

We are twice armed if we fight with faith.

—Plato[9]

CHAPTER 3

God Fulfills Visions

ঈ **Life Question:** What does it take to achieve my dream?

ঈ **Miracle Moment:** The miracle of vision

ঈ **Life Lesson:** God is not a tease.

FOR A MOMENT I WONDERED IF I HAD LOST MY MIND. IT FELT AS if I was stepping into another world—maybe the third heaven? As soon as I saw our treasured spiritual mentor entering our midst, I gasped, "Papa Ward! What are you doing here?" This was impossible! Papa Ward had died four years earlier. I still remembered his funeral service vividly since I sat next to his widow to console her. Yet here he stood at the altar of our camp chapel. Strangely no one else noticed him. I wondered: "How can everyone else overlook a three-hundred-pound man?" I said, "Thank God you're here, Papa," choking back tears. "Tommy and I have never needed advice so much in our entire ministry."

To my dismay Papa Ward ignored me as he picked his way through the crowded chapel, many of the people lost in ecstasy during a praise and worship service. Spotting Tommy, he waddled through the crowd, shaking his head and grumbling, "Can't talk. Can't talk. Business from the other side."

"Papa, we need help," I moaned, yielding to the tears. "We have broken pipes, no tractor, disgruntled pastors, exhausted staff members, and land payments of six thousand dollars a month!"

Still he ignored me.

Poof! Another man materialized in the back corner near Tommy. I recognized him as Virgil Mott Sr., a respected businessman close to our fathers' age; he served the Lord in a different city. Reaching first for Tommy's hand, Papa Ward awkwardly stretched across the aisle to grasp Virgil's hand. Then he gently jerked to join Tommy and Virgil's hands and tilted his head toward heaven. Letting out a belly laugh, he said, "Gotta go. Back to the other side, back to the other side." Poof! Papa vanished.

As I shook my head, the slamming of a car door awakened me from my afternoon nap. Groggy, I was pregnant with our daughter, Abby. When I peered through the upstairs window, my eyes grew wide. There in our driveway, stood Virgil Mott Sr. and his wife, Martha! I knew then that God had given me this special dream and was supernaturally joining Tommy and Virgil for His purposes. For the next twenty-three years Virgil served as a faithful friend, cheerful father in the Lord, savvy businessman, and faithful prayer partner. This experience demonstrates that dreams and visions from the Lord are real. Learn to welcome them.

Half a million wiggly, wonderful kids

CANDIDATE FOR VISIONS

"And it shall come to pass that I will pour out My spirit upon all flesh; and your sons and daughters shall prophesy, your old men shall dream dreams, your young men shall see visions" (Joel 2:28). According to Joel, believers can expect to receive dreams and visions, a primary purpose for the Spirit's outpouring. Most dreams and visions reveal God's heart about a person(s) or place and His plans to bring something to pass. Others are simply revelations of Himself. Visions are real and occur more frequently than you might suspect. Have you ever had a dream or a vision? It may represent divine guidance or insight into a question you have posed. How should you respond? Paul's two questions on the Damascus Road provide the right response: 1) "'Who are You, Lord?'" and 2) "'Lord, what do You want me to do?'" (Acts 9:5–6).

Although a bit of oversimplification, I place visions in four neat categories: 1) the power of imagination, 2) "burning bush" visions, 3) John 16:13 spirit visions, and 4) the John 3:16 vision. Don't search for these personal descriptions in any theological textbooks. (I know that there are prophetic dreams, symbolic dreams, encouraging dreams, and warning dreams, but I find that people tend to complicate things so much they often miss the message entirely.) My understanding stems from more than forty-five years of experience. It works for me. Having said that, regardless of *what* type of vision you experience, it is imperative that *all* dreams and visions agree with the Word of God. Human experience never supersedes the written Word of God. This will become increasingly important as the Day of the Lord approaches and the spirit of deception increases.

VISIONS THROUGH IMAGINATION

Visions come through the mental and spiritual faculties. With honorable motives your power of imagination can bless the world. Such was certainly the case for world-renowned Disneyland in Anaheim,

California. Walt Disney had a vision for a theme park where children and parents could have fun together. The more he dreamed of a "magical park," the more imaginative and elaborate it grew. However, recognize that the fulfillment of most visions takes twice as long and costs twice as much. His original plans for an eight-acre park exploded into 160 acres. That little park turned into a $17 million Magic Kingdom.

In the months preceding Disneyland's grand opening, Walt's dream morphed into a nightmare. His company had to clear away 160 acres of citrus trees and fifteen houses before construction could start. The artificial river called Rivers of America didn't hold water. The Mark Twain riverboat had to come down the Santa Ana freeway deck by deck just so it could make it on time for opening day. Opening ceremonies on July 17, 1955, also proved a disaster. Though Disney mailed 6,000 invitations, 28,000 people arrived with counterfeit tickets. A fifteen-day heat wave had raised temperatures as high as 110 degrees, with still-steaming asphalt trapping ladies' high-heel shoes. Due to a plumbers' strike, few water fountains were operating. Yes, Walt had the right to be discouraged, but he believed in his vision. Within a decade 50 million visitors had passed through Disneyland's gates.[1]

Walt Disney represented one of the twentieth century's greatest visionaries. Sixteen years later, during the opening ceremonies of Disney World in Orlando, company executives invited Walt's widow to cut the ribbon and say a few words. One of the executives remarked, "Mrs. Disney, I wish that Walt could have seen this." Lillian Disney walked over to the podium, adjusted the microphone, and said, "He did." Then she sat down.[2]

To be consumed with a vision is the most wonderful adventure a person can experience. What could be better than to give your life to something you are passionate about? It might be a classroom of toddlers or a political advocacy group. Whatever it is, consider asking the Lord to drop His vision or eternal purpose into your heart, and then: *Run, Forrest, run.* God created our minds with infinite powers, which can be used for positive or negative purposes. Walt Disney is a good example of a man who achieved greatness through the power of imagination.

THE BURNING BUSH

The other three types of visions advance God's purposes and originate in the spirit, starting with what I call the "burning bush." This category includes all types of God-sent dreams or visions. To distinguish, a vision is a supernatural revelation or visitation while you are awake; a dream reveals a message from God while you sleep. Many people in the Bible received a dream or vision from the Lord. Abram had a vision of a burning torch, and Moses saw a burning bush. Joseph dreamt of the stars bowing down to the moon, while Ezekiel saw a wheel in the middle of a wheel. There are at least fifty-five examples in Scripture.[3]

God sent most of the dreams and visions recorded in the Bible to promote His purposes on the earth. Sometimes they provided warnings or protection. Does the Lord ever reveal something trivial—like whether you should move to New Mexico or Alabama? Perhaps, but your chances of hearing from heaven will greatly increase if you align yourself with the purposes of God.

A modern example of big dreamers is Henry Krause. One night in 1938 the Lord gave Krause the design of a revolutionary plow. Engineers in Kansas and Canada called his theory "impossible" since it went against all engineering theories and scientific principles. Although they mocked his invention, Krause built it exactly as his dream revealed. His invention changed the face of wheat country. He became a multimillionaire and donated much of his profits to the Assemblies of God Home Missions Department to build churches.[4]

God also appeared to my husband in January of 1989, three months after we resigned our ministry positions and converted our garage into a prayer room and ministry office. During this time we fielded several opportunities to reach young people via television ministry, national crusades, or developing a retreat center. The latter included some beautiful wooded property in East Texas. One day as Tommy contemplated these offers, he glanced up and saw Jesus—not with his physical eyes, but Tommy discerned where He stood, His height, and His purpose for coming. The Lord said, "Take the camp in Columbus. There's more that I will reveal to you later." Then He smiled and vanished. Tommy could barely speak about this experience, but one look at his face and I knew: *We need to get started.* We moved forward that night by creating a checklist for our seventy-mile move. We had received our divine directive.

A John 16:13 Vision

Don't limit dreams or visions to the "burning bush" category. During prayer the Holy Spirit will show you things to come. I call this a "John 16:13 Vision": "When He, the Spirit of truth, has come, He will guide you into all truth; for He will not speak on His own authority, but whatever He hears He will speak; and He will tell you things to come." In such a vision your spiritual eyes will see something that your natural intellect doesn't. Once you understand this process of spiritual guidance and confirm that it agrees with God's written Word, you will see more with your eyes closed than open.

One of my first such visions came to me in 1974, right before high school graduation. My parents were insisting I follow the path of my two older sisters and attend college. I knew that God had called me into full-time ministry. Kneeling by my bed as I prayed in the Spirit, I had a vision of three pieces of neon, lime-green luggage. Instantly I sensed an inward witness and recognized that I would be traveling extensively. When graduation week arrived, my parents dragged in a huge box and said, "Instead of a giving you a stereo like we gave your sisters, this gift really grabbed our attention." You guessed it: three pieces of bright, lime-green luggage. I used this "John 16:13" luggage two weekends per month as I crisscrossed the nation to share God's love with thousands. (I also honored my parents and completed studies to become a registered nurse.)

While many people are waiting on God, in reality He is waiting on them. A "John 16:13 Vision" comes when God's love to reach people with the gospel compels you to action. Have you ever been in an airport and looked directly into the empty eyes of people rushing nowhere? Are you consumed with a desire to share God's love with them? Bravo. You are allowing the John 16:13 vision to grow within you. As you get consumed with this vision, I guarantee that you will hear from heaven. Abandon yourself to loving the world as God loves the world, and you will be ruined for the ordinary forever.

NURTURING YOUR VISION

"Then the LORD answered me and said: 'Write the vision and make it plain on tablets, that he may run who reads it. For the vision is yet for an appointed time; but at the end it will speak, and it will not lie. Though it tarries, wait for it; because it will surely come, it will not tarry.... But the just shall live by his faith'" (Hab. 2:2–4). Do you have a dream, a goal, or a vision from God? If He gave it to you and you are willing to embrace His promises, you will see it come to fruition. In the meantime here are eight steps to help you nurture it.

STEP 1: Envision it.

I call this the act of living in your future. Can you envision yourself living in your dream? The first step in nurturing the vision is to envision its fulfillment. Imagine it. Embrace it. It wasn't difficult for Tommy and me to see ourselves moving to Country Camp and ministering to young people. That had been our driving purpose during six years together and in our separate ministries before that. You might not transition toward your dream quite as easily. Consider the Israelites who walked through the Red Sea. On one side they had been slaves, but by the time they reached the other side, they should have seen themselves as a chosen, royal nation. Sadly, though it only took one night to get the Israelites out of Egypt, it took forty years to get Egypt out of the Israelites.

To better see the possible, consider Nehemiah, a perfect role model for exemplary, visionary leadership. A political statesman, he served as a cupbearer to Persia's King Artaxerxes (in modern terms, a close advisor to the US president). When distressing news of Jerusalem's devastation reached him, he didn't respond immediately. Too often people make rash moves based on an emotional reaction. Better to be late and in God's will than early and out of it. Nehemiah spent four months fasting, praying, and contemplating his move to Jerusalem.

You can only seize what you see. So stare at the sky and meditate on your dream. See yourself doing what He has called you to do. If He has given you a desire to start your own business, write out your mission statement and design a business card. I have a shoebox filled with paper napkins from restaurants displaying Tommy's now-aged scribbles of artwork, outlines, and projects. As wise Solomon wrote, "For as he thinks in his heart, so is he" (Prov. 23:7).

This stage is vital since it helps you prepare for the inevitable difficult times. This is the season to count the cost, confirm the source, and consider the consequences. Sometimes your heart can get ahead of your head (no pun intended) and prompt you to act impulsively. This is usually a mistake. Our Good Shepherd is never in a hurry. He gently leads—not drives—His sheep. Unless you sense a supernatural direction, stay on the natural path. Spend some time by still waters, pondering, preparing, looking, and living in your future.

Step 2: Adopt tunnel vision.

You must maintain focus to resist distractions and detours. I compare a consuming vision to driving through a tunnel. With nothing on the left or right to distract you, the only direction to go is forward. Tunnel vision preserved our destiny, particularly during our first two years when two other camps offered their property to us. Both were attractive, including one offering a gorgeous hacienda and magnificent views of the Texas Hill Country. We seriously considered operating three camps at once. Fortunately the Holy Spirit exposed them as challenging counterfeits and instructed us to maintain our vision for Discovery Camp.

Nehemiah had this same focus as he rebuilt Jerusalem's walls. Four times when city leaders asked to meet with him, he replied, "I am doing a great work, so that I cannot come down. Why should the work cease while I leave it and go down to you?" (Neh. 6:3). After ninety-four years of failures, Nehemiah's tunnel vision enabled him to complete the project in just fifty-two days. Likewise you need to avoid getting distracted with what may appear to be new, exciting opportunities. Remember, it is not how you *start* your race but how you *finish* that matters. Steady is the new strong. Like a workhorse, put on blinders and plod on.

Step 3: Assemble a team.

To maintain your vision, you need to assemble a team that surrounds and supports it. With every great vision God raises up a supporting team. Nehemiah knew that he couldn't fulfill his vision to rebuild the walls of Jerusalem by himself. So he brought a team with him and convinced them that they could accomplish this task. Nehemiah said that God gave them "a mind to work" (Neh. 4:6) twelve-hour shifts with such passionate loyalty that they slept in their work clothes.

There are those who receive a vision and others who give themselves to it. Some are called to lead; others are called to follow. The presence of loyal team players and committed followers is God's gift to a visionary. Such people are no less valuable. They are graced with the ability to serve, trust, and fulfill their role. Proverbs says,

"Where there is no vision, the people perish" (Prov. 29:18, KJV), but it is equally accurate to say, "Without people, the vision perishes."

I firmly believe special rewards await our loyal staff once they reach heaven. Several have served beside us for twenty-five years, forsaking their own plans for a higher calling. People often ask, "What is your secret for success?" The answer: S-W-E-A-T. There is no substitute for a strong work ethic. Our staff reminds me of the old farmer who spent nine laborious months developing several acres of neglected farmland. When a pastor from a nearby city came to visit, he exclaimed, "What a great job you've done making the Lord's farm so beautiful." Replied the farmer: "Thanks, but you should have seen it when the Lord had it all by Himself."

One busy weekend I saw an employee who had been working nonstop to get a plumbing dilemma fixed. He looked so frustrated and tired, I said, "Thank you for working so hard. Why don't you take the rest of the weekend off?" Looking confused, he replied, "Why would I do that? We have nine hundred teenagers here who are meeting Jesus. This is what we live for!" To be in leadership here requires a person to act as a builder. Some of our staff build bunk beds and some sermons, but we are all committed to build up visiting churches and their young people.

STEP 4: Communicate the vision.

Your goal is not just to receive a great vision but also to persuade others to adopt it as their own. I cannot overstate your need to speak passionately and effectively about your vision. If you will learn to act pro-vision, you will never lack provision. I have sometimes doodled on papers listening to businessmen and missionaries blab on and on about their respective projects. An hour later I still can't quite grasp what they do. To repeat Habakkuk's counsel, "Write the vision and make it plain" (Hab. 2:2). Our vision themes for our camp, school, and church:

+ Discovery Camp: A friend to the local church

+ Texas Bible Institute: Laying strong foundations for life

+ Believers World Outreach Church: A family church
  with a heart for the world

Write it and rewrite it until you get it exactly right. Practice saying it with enthusiasm. Leadership expert John Maxwell says, "A great leader's courage to fulfill his vision comes from passion, not position."[5] If you're not excited, why should anyone join you? Instead of saying something like, "We really need your help in the youth department," try saying, "There is someone here who will discover— by investing just one hour per week—the joy of making a difference in the future of our young people. Is that someone you?"

Trained salespersons can provide insights about sharing vision. A good one knows that instead of selling you a mattress, they are marketing a peaceful night's sleep. They don't offer aspirin; instead, they describe pain relief. Ask yourself: What benefit is there for someone to join my vision? Jack Welch, the former General Electric chairman and CEO, once said, "Good business leaders create a vision, articulate the vision, passionately own the vision and relentlessly drive it to completion."[6]

Our visionary hero Nehemiah knew how to inspire others. How else can you explain him persuading more than one hundred people to travel nine hundred miles through deserts full of thieves and wild animals on an unpredictable journey? That would be like walking from Houston, Texas, to Atlanta, Georgia. Listen to his pro-vision words: "Then I said to them, 'You see the distress that we are in, how Jerusalem lies waste, and its gates are burned with fire. Come and let us build the wall of Jerusalem, that we may no longer be a reproach'" (Neh. 2:17–18). Their response appears in the last half of verse 18: "So they said, 'Let us rise up and build.' Then they set their hands to this good work."

STEP 5: Commit yourself to excellence.

Executing a vision requires a commitment to excellence. Everything done for the Lord should be done with excellence. An emphasis on "the anointing" should not be a ready excuse for sloppiness or lack of organization. People would be surprised to see how much organization goes on behind the scenes of our Spirit-led ministry. It often can be characterized as "Make a list, meet with executives, and send a memo."

Just as real ministry is tough work, precision is imperative if you hope to see your vision fulfilled. For example, our events department makes hundreds of phone calls to visiting churches so we don't wind up with 1,200 campers arriving to sleep in 1,000 beds. If the water sports department miscalculates the chlorine and cyanuric acid going into our covered swimming pool and 3 waterslides, campers will find a "closed" sign on them. Our 80 air conditioners need regular servicing, as do 174 toilets. At the conclusion of every camp session, a team of interns wipes down both sides of 1,000 mattresses with an ammonium disinfectant. These duties must be handled with diligence and precision. We don't need the Holy Spirit to lead us through every detail. Understanding stewardship and responsibility provides the bulk of our job descriptions.

We employ one hundred Texas Bible Institute alumni each summer at our massive Discovery Camps. Filled with zeal and loyalty, these interns are the greatest kids on the planet. They work with a "green light" mentality and learn the joy of working heartily as unto the Lord. However, since it is often their first *real* job, competence is typically an issue. Our patient supervisors find themselves fixing and redoing simple tasks. One July morning we walked into our ice cream store, The Chill, to find one hundred fifty gallons of melted ice cream—the result of a well-meaning staffer unplugging the freezer to wax the floor. Another young man in the kitchen accidentally put salt instead of sugar into the peach cobbler. Vision needs precision.

Step 6: Make good decisions.

When accomplishing your dream, wise decision making is significant. There are two schools of thought here. The first, which I gravitate toward, is to *do something* lest you *do nothing*. Tommy embraces a much different style of leadership, preferring to ponder every action and reaction as if he were playing a painfully slow game of chess. I call it his tiger dance, where he slowly circles a decision and then pounces. (While both styles are fine, his is probably better.) Whichever style you prefer, you must brace yourself for reactions from those who do not know the entire story. Acting as a velvet-covered brick is not for the faint of heart. You must remain tender with people yet inwardly committed to your core convictions. When making a tough decision, ask yourself these questions:

+ Will it advance the vision?

+ Will the rippling effects be short-term or long-term?

+ Is this the best time to face the repercussions, or would postponing it minimize the effects?

Strong character will lead most of your decisions. Leaders do what's right, when it's right, just because it's right. Hold your head high and keep your standards high as you live for that day of fulfillment.

Step 7: Make necessary adjustments.

I call this the "re-visioning process." This doesn't signal surrender but that life tends to bring surprises that demand revisions. I recently read about a woman who had hopes of her daughter becoming a *prima ballerina*, the most notable of female ballet dancers. On her daughter's third birthday Mom enrolled her in her first class. The grueling lessons continued for ten years, until the slim girl's preteen hormones kicked in. By her fourteenth birthday she was five feet and nine inches, with a thick waist and large ankles.

By fifteen she exchanged toe shoes for basketball sneakers and ultimately progressed to the collegiate level.

Life always offers surprises. I admit it: some of my great visions were disasters. My Discovery Camp post-worship service "kum-bah-yah devotionals" gradually shifted into late-night waterslide parties. We routinely ask, "How can we make this better without losing the objective of the vision?" This isn't an embarrassment, considering that Nehemiah revised his strategy. Chapter four of his narrative describes how discouragement and weariness affected his workers, so he completely revamped work schedules and changed some job descriptions.

The most significant revision in our story came when Tommy announced to our staff that he would be preaching only the last two nights of each camp. This concept was inconceivable to our partner churches. My husband *was* Discovery Camp! Many told us they came so their youth could benefit from Pastor Tommy's anointing. While leadership manuals teach that no one is indispensable, Tommy might have been the exception. Big ships turn slowly, so when you make revisions, try to make them gradually. Today it has been more than a decade since Tommy ministered at camp youth rallies; most kids today wouldn't even recognize him. Instead he is usually at his legendary leaders' meetings, imparting inspiration and information to a new generation.

Step 8: Remain balanced.

To fulfill your dream you need a "double vision," meaning you must maintain a balance between practical and spiritual goals. I realize it sounds like a contradiction to simultaneously embrace tunnel vision and double vision. However, if you intend to run a marathon instead of a sprint, both are necessary. I am referring to your private and public lives. Visionaries who are consumed with God's zeal need to keep their personal life strong. Just as a bird with one wing cannot fly, neither can a vision without a healthy visionary. You must separate your vision from your personal life for two reasons. First of all, ministry demands will drain you of the stamina and creative juices needed to sustain the vision. Secondly, if you hope to see your vision outlive you, you need to detach it from your personality.

Granted, Nehemiah maintained tunnel vision for fifty-two days. But if you read more closely, you will see he had a wife, a family, and the luxurious life of a governor. The dedication ceremonies for the wall's completion included numerous parties and festivities. We have every reason to believe that he took his family on some getaway weekends in the beautiful land of Israel. You might say, "Rachel, the Bible doesn't say that he did that." True, but it doesn't say that he didn't either.

Think of your vision as a pregnancy. Your intimacy with God caused its conception; through your labor it came forth. But that is the easy part. During infancy a baby demands your full attention, but by the time she is five years old, you should be able to take a peaceful nap. By the time she reaches ten, you should be able to leave her with a babysitter overnight. You are the parental voice who provides direction, which is all the more reason you must stay fresh. If you burn your candle at both ends, you will have nothing left. Be disciplined to nurture a hobby or recreational outlet while fulfilling your vision. Tommy and I, and the camp supervisors, learned this lesson the hard way. Pace yourself.

THE NIGHTMARE PHASE

Our vision to reach and disciple young people has been like an epic film that requires an extended intermission. We are honored beyond words that God chose us to play a role in His master plan, but occasionally the dream has been a nightmare.

For example, to briefly describe our first summer, we only had three weeks to prepare the neglected grounds and renovate five buildings for the two thousand campers we expected. Previously Country Camp had been family-owned and operated, with beds for two hundred. Though we had no cook, no staff, no mechanics, and no electricians, we reasoned that we had a God-given dream and the Holy Ghost's anointing. Yet the grass stood so tall that Andrew (nearly three) got lost for a few minutes in a pasture looking for his ball. A small band of friends had moved with us from Houston and slept in old trailers or the barn. Our first camp administrator and worship leader slept in a walk-in closet. Tommy spent much of his time on a tractor, while I stayed busy creating curriculum and decorating the little chapel. It seemed as though well-meaning "helpers" broke everything they tried to fix. Add in sixteen-hour days, and we could have easily yielded to discouragement, just as we could have for those unjust accusations over an employee's dismissal.

However, this is life. You must learn to take the bad along with the good. Fortunately, despite those oft-trying early days, we kept going because we recognized that Jesus had given us an opportunity to help young people and their leaders. Such recognition kept us from growing weary.

THE BURCHFIELD HOTEL

One morning during prayer in those early days the Lord asked me if I would open my home with the same passion that I had opened my heart to Him years before. I should have known that He had something up His sleeve. When I promised to "bless them as they come in and bless them when they leave," He replied, "They're not leaving." As the word got out that Tommy and Rachel had their own camp, the phone started ringing. Moms volunteered to cook and licensed electricians and certified lifeguards showed up. Every detail seemed divinely orchestrated.

The main problem, as I already mentioned, stemmed from our limited housing. Tommy wasn't about to let that stop him. He came into the house one afternoon all excited.

"Sug, Annie and Sandy can stay all summer to help," he said.

"Can they stay in our house?" I quickly consented. The next day Tommy changed the names but made the same request. Once again, grateful for the help, I consented. Day after day the list of my "summertime daughters" grew. Girls I didn't even know were knocking on my door with suitcases in tow saying, "Brother Tommy told me that I would be staying here. I'm Cheryl." We topped out at thirty teenage girls living upstairs and sleeping two to a bed, with bunk beds in the hallways and one girl camped out in the bathtub! It was a wonderful, chaotic experience that I never want to repeat.

These were young people who took us literally when we said, "God's not looking for ability but availability." Though few were skilled, how precious was their zeal!

One day a helper called to ask, "Brother Tommy, do you know where Dorm C is?" "Yes," he replied.

"You know where that wall was by the parking lot? Well, it's not there anymore."

Brent, our fifteen-year-old "staff" member, had driven the ministry truck smack dab into the wall. That is when Tommy remarked, "If this camp is going to survive, we've got to teach these kids how to drive!" The next week Tommy announced he was going to build a figure eight, double-looped go-cart track. And he did. While you may not encounter the same nutty circumstances, you will face trials. Be careful not to major on the nightmare phase of your dream. Stay focused on the One who entrusted it to you. What He begins, He will complete. Wait for it. Fight for it. Believe in it. That is what Tommy and I did, and we are now living our dream. Some day you too will smile and say, along with the great poet Edwin Markham, "Ah, great it is to believe the dream as we stand in youth by the starry stream; but a greater thing is to fight life through and say at the end, the dream is true!"[7]

Swimming pools, archery, horses, and gooooo-carts

THE MIRACLE OF VISION

Some people see things as they are and ask why. I dream things that never were and say, "Why not?"

—George Bernard Shaw[8]

People with vision see the invisible, believe the incredible and do the impossible.

—Tommy Burchfield[9]

To grasp and hold a vision is the very essence of successful leadership.

—Ronald Reagan[10]

If you can dream it, you can do it....this whole thing was started by a mouse.

—Walt Disney[11]

If your dreams don't scare you, you're probably dreaming too small.

—Wayne Myers[12]

It takes twenty years to become an overnight success.

—Author unknown

CHAPTER 4

Suicides and Setbacks

&❧ **Life Question:** Where is God in my pain?

&❧ **Miracle Moment:** The miracle of hope

&❧ **Life Lesson:** God can turn tragedy into triumph.

JIM (A PSEUDONYM) REPRESENTED THE KIND OF YOUNG PERSON WE hoped to reach when we moved to Columbus in the spring of 1989. We came to train, equip, and encourage teens to reach the world for Christ, as well as help those struggling with life's challenges, uncertainties, and setbacks. Our guiding philosophy throughout our ministry has been: *Give young people a vision and watch them soar.* God has given Tommy and me an anointing to understand them and a grace to believe in them. Many young people with the most hopeless set of circumstances have blossomed into productive, strong Christian leaders. Yet others who had the benefit of growing up in a stable home environment still shipwrecked later in life.

Granted, Jim had endured some obstacles along the way. Yet over the years his lovely, godly mother had driven him and his older brother many miles to participate in our outreach events. When Jim moved to the camp to join our staff, he gave every indication that he was about to soar. Working diligently in the camp kitchen and playing the drums during worship services, he made us beam with pride at his progress—particularly since we had personal knowledge of the setbacks he had to overcome to make it this far.

July 22, 1992, started out like most days that summer. Nine hundred teenagers gathered for breakfast while wearing colored name badges, as they always did. As usual, youth pastors chatted with them over bacon and eggs while boasting of their volleyball victories. Those involved in the Team Talent Quest dragged their door-sized props out of church vans, another customary camp scene. Afterward Jim played the drums during worship as he always did while the nine o'clock ministry team powerfully shared God's love.

However, this morning two unusual things took place. First, the praise leader felt prompted by the Holy Spirit to offer a prayer time at the conclusion of the service. This was a unique occurrence at the morning service, when sleepy campers are still coming to life and spiritual leaders operate at a lower energy level too. It was even more unusual for someone on the stage to stand and request prayer. Still, it never struck us as that extraordinary. Nor did we suspect Jim's inability to deal with reality as he stood by his drums and bowed his head in silence.

Our original chapel in 1989

SHOCKING DISCOVERY

When Jim failed to report for kitchen duty two hours later, another teen dashed to his room to check on him and scold him for "dogging it." Instead, to his shock and dismay, he discovered Jim's lifeless body on the floor with a single bullet wound on the left side of his head. A .38-caliber automatic handgun lay on the floor. The rock music of Stryper blared across the death-filled bedroom. *Suicide.* More than twenty years later the details reverberate through everyone's mind. We still wonder how Jim, who genuinely loved Jesus, couldn't find the power to deal with some of life's major disappointments.

The next forty-eight hours brought a whirlwind of sheriff's deputies, ambulances, and phone calls, as well as a defining moment in the lives of two heartbroken leaders with the reputation for building and believing in young people. Most people never knew this incident represented a sudden and all-too-soon *déjà vu* moment. In the past year we had buried a family friend after a similar tragedy. Two suicides of born-again Christians in such a short time? Although there was clearly something terribly with this picture, time didn't allow us the luxury of processing those unspoken concerns.

Tommy plowed into handling the grueling details ahead and asked me to take over the responsibilities of keeping the Discovery Camp program moving forward. Although I nodded my assent, my insides churned as questions rocketed through my mind: *What do I do? What do I say? Can anything good come from such heartbreak?* We had nine hundred teenagers from forty-two churches attending this particular camp. Many had heard the ambulance sirens and seen our hysterical, sobbing staff. News of Jim's death spread like wildfire, along with rumors, questions, and false accusations. Despite his rash action, Jim didn't fit the mold of a dysfunctional misfit. A popular young man searching for difficult answers, he didn't take time to find them. As with everyone who checks

out in such a manner, the answer is that he *gave up too quickly.*
Although I gathered our staff privately to give them instructions,
I wrestled internally with doubts and groped for the right words.
At that moment none of our *Conflict and Crisis Resolution* outlines
seemed appropriate. So I prayed: "Lord, what do I say?" Suddenly
the promise of hope found in Romans rushed into my spirit. In an
instant I found immediate clarity (when you are in leadership, you
can expect the Holy Spirit to lead you that easily). Paul's promise
took on new meaning in the depths of our despair: "And we know
that all things work together for good to those who love God, to
those who are called according to His purpose" (Rom. 8:28).

Although in those moments we struggled with seeing what
good could come from this, together we dedicated ourselves to winning souls in Jim's memory and asked God to turn this tragedy into
triumph. I said the only prayer I knew to lead our grieving staff:
"Father, You have promised that 'all things work together for good,'
so on behalf of this dear soul who prematurely stepped into eternity,
we are asking for a harvest of souls." After a box of Kleenex made
the rounds, I pushed about ten staff members onto the stage with
this challenge: "Be strong in the Lord."

As the campers gathered for the evening Miracle Rally, they
noticed someone else had taken Jim's position at the drums. I felt
such a responsibility to tell them the truth without ruining their
annual camp visit. Breathing deeply, I smiled courageously and
said, "Jesus loves each of you so much. Usually He brings you to
Discovery Camp to be blessed. But during this year's visit He also
wants you to become a blessing to others. Right now I need to
make an announcement that's very difficult, and your Discovery
Camp staff sure does need your prayers. Our camp family has
experienced a tragedy today. The reason Jim is not by his drums
right now is because he is no longer with us. As some of you

probably knew, Jim died this morning, but he is alive forever in the presence of the Lord."

I did not give any further details, but I explained that the promises of God could carry them through every crisis and challenged both campers and staff to postpone their soul-searching questions to believe for a Romans 8:28 triumph. Oh! What an anointing fell over those campers as I passionately asked, "If you had been the one who died today, where would you spend eternity?" Troubled teens flooded to the altar and found comfort in a loving Father. Many accepted Jesus as their Savior that night and committed themselves to become soulwinners, taking seriously the eternal destinations of their family and friends.

GOD'S ODD QUESTION

As we drove one hundred fifty miles to officiate at Jim's funeral, an odd event occurred. Tommy glanced toward the side of the interstate and saw a huge, abandoned, double-looped waterslide. A sign beside it contained a phone number to call for more information. Though pretty occupied with the seriousness of Jim's home-going service, Tommy was stunned when this message resounded in his spirit: "If you want it, you can have it." How peculiar to hear a clear word from God at such a sad moment. Yet the Lord had begun turning this tragedy into triumph, just as our heartbroken staff had prayed.

For the next several days that specific phrase thundered inside Tommy's spirit: "If you want it, you can have it." We did want it! We chuckled over the humorous mental picture of such a huge contraption plunked down in the middle of a 553-acre cow pasture. But we knew that action-packed fun provides incredible bait for young people. Knowing the Bible principle that faith moves forward, we called the number on the sign and learned that a successful banker owned it. We arranged a meeting. Tommy and I took one of our project managers with us, a guy I'll call Ted, since he had some (emphasis on *some*) business and building experience. During a rather brief meeting the businessman explained, "Tommy, I was just sure this venture would fly. I sank $365,000 into this water park and hit a dead end. Why, it's become such an eyesore to me that I'd almost give it to you."

We hardly breathed for the remainder of the twenty-minute discussion. When he asked why we wanted it so badly, Tommy's heart to reach children and teenagers with God's love shone brightly. It felt like the Holy Spirit stepped into the room and put on the best presentation in history! When Tommy finished, the banker said, "Well, it seems like a formidable task to me, but *if you want it, you can have it.*" The last phrase ricocheted through our minds, since they were the same exact words Jesus used!

"Do you know how to get it dismantled and transported one hundred fifty miles?" the man asked.

"Oh, yes sir!" replied my visionary Tommy. "That's why we brought Ted with us."

All the way home we laughed and cried. We cried because we recognized God had quickly started turning Jim's tragedy into a triumph. We laughed because our poor project manager didn't have a clue how to transport it back to Columbus. Yet, several months later, our one-thousand-foot-long double-loop Miracle Waterslide sat scattered across our volleyball courts in hundreds of carefully marked pieces.

"This is a no-brainer," our project manager boasted as his assistants nodded in a silent chorus of affirmation. "It's just like putting together a giant LEGO kit." However, soon after they didn't feel so smug when a Texas gully-washer flushed away the chalk numbers. After purchasing a can of spray paint, the crisis crumbled— and the men felt humbled. They also decided they had better look to the Lord to reconstruct this metal, soul-winning machine.

Everything they set out to accomplish seemed to take twice as long as planned.

First, they had to grind off seven thousand rusted bolts with helpers that included teenage homeschoolers, good-hearted handymen, and a few ladies who patiently sanded and resanded every piece several times. When the main contractor angrily ditched the job, God sent us experts to erect the fifty-two-foot-tall structure and laborers to complete it. Our staff tested it late one night "in memory of their friend Jim."

That event more than twenty years ago remains as a structural testimony of Romans 8:28. No, it didn't bring Jim back to us, but it has enticed many of the more than five hundred thousand campers we have hosted to travel to Texas from twenty-nine states, enjoy the fun, and meet Jesus as their personal Lord and Savior. This memory relates vividly to something that happened during an early-morning devotional session before the tragedy of Jim's suicide. As my morning coffee percolated and I searched for my "#1 Mom" cup and favorite Bible verse of the week, I rehearsed these three thoughts:

1. Since God is in control, I don't need to apply.

2. Today is a good day for a miracle.

3. He is my strength in the "day of trouble."

I highly recommend keeping these points in front of you and meditating on them regularly. Since each new day brings its own set of problems and pleasures, it is beneficial to get spiritually prepared before you blast off, especially if you're working with young people. Because we had daily embraced the strength of God, Jim's death did not prove a knockout punch for us. God brought us through our day of trouble and gave us something to talk about by working everything for good.

The Day of Trouble

A portion of your human experience will include shocking episodes such as Jim's death. When calamity strikes, it will be what numerous Bible passages refer to as the "day of trouble"—a time when life's circumstances create an opportunity for hopelessness and despair. Yet it is also an opportunity for your faith, which is more precious than gold, to become strong and pure. Jesus prepared us for these difficult moments when He said, "In this world, you will have tribulation; but be of good cheer; I have overcome the world" (John 16:33). Neither the godly nor ungodly are immune to problems, but believers get to remain victorious all the way through them. Job is an example of a godly man who experienced a horrible day of trouble, yet it didn't last forever. Religious people imply that he was miserable throughout his life, but that is not the case. Most Bible scholars believe his trials lasted only nine months. Nine months! In addition, in the end God blessed him with twice as much as before the crisis.

There is a proper response to such difficult times, however, so that it will thrust you into victory and not destruction. Do not fear or dread the day of trouble, whether it lasts a few days or a few years. If you resist fear and respond in faith, eventually it will become a day of triumph. As you learn to respond in faith instead of fear, God will show Himself mighty on your behalf. You can draw encouragement from the fact that such setbacks don't take God by surprise and that you will survive. As you worship Jesus your refuge, you will not only survive but also eventually thrive. Don't allow your day of trouble to get the best of you; the Holy Spirit has empowered you to get on top of it. As Paul wrote, "Now thanks be to God who always leads us in triumph in Christ" (2 Cor. 2:14).

While the Book of Psalms contains sixteen references to a day of (or times of) trouble, it also has sixty-eight references to hope.

These scriptures of hope reveal that God is with us in our trouble, revealing Himself as our refuge who provides strength, comfort, and deliverance. Consider just a few of them:

- ✦ "Call upon Me in the day of trouble; I will deliver you, and you shall glorify Me" (Ps. 50:15).

- ✦ "I will sing of Your power; yes, I will sing aloud of Your mercy in the morning; for You have been my defense and refuge in the day of my trouble" (Ps. 59:16).

- ✦ "In the day of my trouble I sought the Lord" (Ps. 77:2).

- ✦ "In the day of my trouble, I will call upon You, for You will answer me" (Ps. 86:7)

- ✦ "Trouble and anguish have overtaken me, yet Your commandments are my delights" (Ps. 119:143).

These psalms, with their emotional ups and downs, remind me of a roller coaster that I endured at Disneyland in Anaheim, California. At the end of the two-minute-and-forty-five-second ride comes a 15-foot drop at 30.2 miles per hour—a cruel blend of exhilaration and suffocation. I clung to the young man in the seat next to me as he held tightly to me so I wouldn't fall out and meet an untimely demise. (Thankfully I was clinging to our oldest son, Andrew.) To survive the 3,035 feet of unexpected twists and turns, I found myself chanting a mantra, "It's only a ride. It will soon be over. It's only a ride. It will soon be over."

If you're in the middle of a day of trouble, cling to God's Word so He can stabilize your emotional ups and downs. Hang on. Eventually that roller coaster will stop, and you will be able to get off and brag about the One who held you tightly.

KNOCKED DOWN, NOT OUT

In their younger years our three children loved playing with a clown-faced, inflatable toy that stood about three feet tall and teetered back and forth. When you punched its smiling face, down to the ground it went before bouncing right back up, thanks to a weighted attachment on the bottom. Regardless of how hard or how often the kids punched it, the smiling clown would always bounce back up. You can enjoy this kind of resiliency due to the victories Jesus won for you at Calvary. Life might knock you down, but the Word will cause you to bounce right back up, because God's Word puts a fight inside your spirit.

Some people try to act as if they never have any problems because their faith is so strong. Right. That isn't reality. Throughout Scripture we see people lamenting their woes—meditate on some of David's psalms and you will see "woe is me" to the max! Or look at the prophet Nahum, who acknowledged he experienced difficulties when he wrote: "The LORD is good, a *stronghold in the day of trouble*; and He knows those who trust in Him" (Nah. 1:7, emphasis added).

Nahum's words give us answers to three of life's most difficult questions:

+ Did God do this? (No, He is a good God.)

+ Where is God in my pain? (He is holding on to you.)

+ What does He want from me? (He is inviting you to trust Him, so that He can show Himself strong on your behalf.)

Notice that Nahum didn't write, "The Lord is your stronghold *from* the day of trouble," but "*in* the day of trouble." Everyone has such a day, but it won't destroy you unless you allow it. Here are three settle-it-forever statements that will give the devil a black eye. They make divine knockout punches every time.

KNOCKOUT PUNCH #1: The Lord is good.

Blaming God is far too many people's initial reaction to bad news. They scream, "Why did God do this?" or "Why did He let this happen?" God didn't send tragedy into your life. God is a good God. He loves you. You will need to settle the goodness of God before you can move forward. Remember, God doesn't send sickness and tornadoes to make people get closer to Him. When Hurricane Katrina hit the Gulf Coast on August 29, 2005, it killed more than 1,800 people[1] and displaced almost 400,000 residents of the Gulf Coast.[2]

In its aftermath I listened to a radio station as a reporter interviewed a woman who lost her two teenagers, her home, and all material possessions. I cringed as she told the reporter, "God has been trying to get my attention for a while, but now I guess I need to listen."[3] No. No. No. A thousand times, no! Please don't blame God for such devastation. God is a good God. Only goodness can come from Him. Why would anyone even want to get close to a God who sent a hurricane that brought such destruction?

Jesus said, "The thief does not come except to steal, and to kill, and to destroy. I have come that they may have life, and that they may have it more abundantly" (John 10:10). Those words make for pretty straightforward theology: Satan is bad. God is good. That is not to say that only good things happen in this world. Keep in mind that some of the natural laws that God set in place were contaminated through the fall of mankind and the deterioration that followed. Nevertheless, God's character has never changed. Settle in your heart forever that the Lord is good.

KNOCKOUT PUNCH #2: The Lord is your stronghold.

In biblical days a stronghold or strong tower served as a fortified place. It functioned as a refuge—a place of security, survival, and safety. When calamity comes, you can run into God's stronghold. As the psalmist wrote, "For You have been a shelter for me, a strong tower from the enemy" (Ps. 61:3). You can literally hide in God's strength. You can probably picture a medieval castle with its large stone towers and drawbridge, but that might prompt the question, "How exactly do I hide in the Lord?" There are several answers, but it may help to metaphorically name three of those medieval towers to give you a clear word picture.

The stronghold of praise

Enter into the first tower, named "praise and worship." There you will find Paul and Silas. While in prison for preaching the gospel, they sang praises at midnight (Acts 16). An earthquake released them from captivity and brought salvation to the jailer's entire family. We have learned to hide in this tower. One time a young camper from Arizona fell off his bunk bed headfirst onto concrete; our resident EMT knew to call 911. A Life Flight helicopter landed in our pasture and at first attempted to take him ninety miles to Austin. Due to dense fog controllers diverted him two hundred miles to Galveston, Texas. While doctors gave our twelve-year-old guest an extremely negative medical report, our amazing staff dedicated themselves to praise and worship. While carrying on daily operations, we strategically kept our hearts filled with praise. Against all odds our little camper came out of the hospital three days later with no injuries. Praise is a weapon!

The stronghold of the altar

Another tower that you can hide in during your day of trouble is the Lord's altar. This is another place where God will become your stronghold. When Hezekiah received an evil letter filled with threats from a neighboring tribe, he took that letter and laid it before the altar of the Lord (2 Kings 18–19). Resisting despair, he committed the situation to Jehovah Nissi, the God who conquers. Hezekiah received divine guidance during his day of trouble and ultimately enjoyed a great victory.

I know going to the altar is a place of refuge because of something that occurred in November of 2011. One Wednesday night I challenged our Believers World Outreach Church family to do exactly what Hezekiah did. They brought a host of negative letters from their doctors, lawyers, bankers, school counselors, and others. This veritable cornucopia of bad news contained diagnoses of terminal illness, divorce, foreclosure warnings, problem grades—they covered the spectrum. Then members spread them across the altar as we sought God for miracles. Rather than yield to fear, we committed them to the Lord. We trusted His Word, which says that He can "keep what I have committed to Him until that Day" (2 Tim. 1:12). Despite the odds, in the weeks and months that followed we witnessed numerous miracles as many of those bad reports turned into good ones.

The stronghold of serving

Although there are many others, the last tower I will elaborate on is the stronghold of serving. Think of the young woman named Ruth, who experienced the fears common during her era. When her husband died, she found herself sixty miles from the security of her own family and people. Consider the despair and hopelessness of being a young widow in another country. Women were utterly dependent on the generosity and provision of men. There were no life insurance policies, no steady income, and no cell phones to call home. Yet, as Ruth threw herself into serving her mother-in-law and her relative, Boaz, God provided her with a new purpose and abundant provision. She and Boaz wound up in the lineage of Christ.

Serving others during your day of trouble allows His perspective to gain clarity in your life. Learn to hide in these strongholds until the battle is over and it is safe to emerge. What is the stronghold? It is either a place of safety or a person who has a strong hold on you. Thankfully in your day of trouble you can apply both to the Lord Jesus. Hiding in the strongholds of the Lord provides a security that unbelievers know nothing about.

KNOCKOUT PUNCH #3: The Lord wants your trust.

When you are walking through your day of trouble, it is common to wonder why you are experiencing such despair. After all, if God is never the source of sickness, misery, or suffering, why did this happen? What does He want? What is He looking for? To summarize briefly my response: All He wants is your trust. He alone is faithful, dependable, and trustworthy.

As you move toward emotional wholeness, you need to say good-bye to all your "whys" and "whats" as you learn to move from "why" to "what now." Instead of meditating on your questions and doubts, meditate on the Word. You will find that God releases a sustaining strength into your spirit. As you trust Him with your unanswered questions and tormenting trials, frequently whisper this simple prayer, "Lord, help me trust You." He will do just that. As He brings you through your day of trouble, you will see the truth about His dependability:

- ✦ Can you trust in His omniscience? Yes, because He sees your dilemma from the throne's view.

- ✦ Can you trust in His kindness? Absolutely. He will carry you until you can walk on your own.

- ✦ Can you trust in His omnipotence? Oh yeah. He will disintegrate any obstacle that hinders His perfect plan for you. Just ask Paul and Silas, Hezekiah, or

Ruth, and they will all shout with overwhelming joy (and relief) that God can be trusted.

Are you ready to knock out the despair and hopelessness associated with setbacks, crisis, and tragedy? Put on your imaginary boxing gloves and notice the promise printed across each one. The left glove says "Nahum 1:7" and the right glove says "Romans 8:28." Those two truths alone will carry you through any day of trouble and fill your life with hope. Remember, your elder Brother, Jesus, has already won the boxing match, but you can still wear those gloves as a souvenir to remember the victory.

THE MIRACLE OF HOPE

If you are in the midst of a trial, I know how you feel. The day of Jim's suicide I struggled to see how good could emerge from such darkness. But if you meditate on Romans 8:28 and embrace its truth, you will find a comfort and a peace that passes all understanding. Please note this amazing promise is reserved for those who love God. If you love God, you can have hope even during your most difficult moments. If you trust Him, He can take a mess and turn it into a miracle. As I wrote these words, I prayed for each person who would read them, and I am expecting Him to perform miracles in your life.

Our home, which I've named Great Oaks, is decorated with my maternal grandmother's beautiful stitchery. My favorite is a multicolored bell pole edged with an ornate, gold-scrolling pattern. Upon restoring the torn fabric on the back, I noticed that the reverse side of this threaded masterpiece contained an ugly combination of knotted thread. Isn't that a lovely example of Romans 8:28? No matter how ugly life may become, the Master can turn it into a beautiful picture. You can have a confident expectation that all things will eventually become good because you have a Father

God who loves you. As Elisabeth Elliot so courageously said many years after the Auca Indians killed her missionary husband, "Anything, if offered to God, can and will become your gateway to joy."[4] Clearly she also embraced the miracle moment of hope.

Years later Tommy and I have embraced hope concerning Jim. We believe, because he truly loved Jesus, that Jim is not just part of our past but also part of our future as well. This is the kind of blessed hope Jesus offers.

*Our awesome staff serve seven hundred
church groups in ten weeks.*

THE MIRACLE OF HOPE

Life at times appears to fall into pieces, seems irreparable. But it's going to be okay. How can you know? Because *God* so loved the world.

—Max Lucado[5]

Hope is patience with the lamp lit.

—Tertullian[6]

God is the only one who can make the valley of trouble a door of hope.

—Catherine Marshall[7]

I've read the last page of the Bible. It's all going to turn out all right.

—Billy Graham[8]

The blood of the martyrs is the seed of the church.

—Tertullian[9]

CHAPTER 5

The Miracle Message

๑ **Life Question:** What is my life message?

๑ **Miracle Moment:** The miracle of the gospel

๑ **Life Lesson:** Miracles are God's amen to the gospel.

ONE OF SATAN'S LEADING TRICKS TO RENDER THE BODY OF CHRIST powerless is to divide and conquer. If the devil can get us fighting and quarreling with one another, shouting and screaming as we argue over denominational distinctives or theological interpretations, we spend less time overcoming the enemy. Today, regardless of where in the world one lives, the church desperately needs to be unified. As believers we need to major on what unites us, not stand on the one soapbox guaranteed to antagonize others. A mixed message brings confusion.

This is quite relevant in our world. Since Discovery Campers come to South Texas from seven hundred church groups, they represent many "camps." In order to unify them, we challenge them to metaphorically drop their church name at the back door so that together we can lift up the one name that will hold us together: Jesus. Don't you agree? We all have so much to contribute to one another, something I have seen lived out in my own life.

After all, I grew up in a Methodist church, accepted Jesus at a Campus Crusade for Christ (now known as Cru) rally, received the baptism of the Holy Spirit at a meeting sponsored by Full

Gospel Business Men's Fellowship International, and married an Assemblies of God minister who later migrated to a Word of Faith church. One of my brothers-in-law is a Baptist minister. I have seen strengths and weaknesses in each group. I think we can agree that we should all get along.

Sometimes the divisions within Christianity frustrate me beyond words. They remind me of the familiar Indian proverb about four blind men who were asked to describe an elephant:

The first man touched the elephant's leg and compared it to a tree trunk.

"No, an elephant is much larger than that," said the second as he rubbed the animal's body. "It is more like a large football.

"You're both wrong," snapped the third as he held the trunk. "An elephant is like a large hose."

Holding the elephant's tail and now quite aggravated, the fourth scoffed, "What's wrong with you idiots? The elephant is much like a small rope."

Each described the elephant from his personal perspective. Isn't this a good picture of the mixed messages spread among believers? There are many rooms in God's house: a prophetic room, an apostolic room, and another for Word of Faith people. Some have experienced the "rooted and fruited" tribe while others are swimming in the river of the Spirit or learning to be still before the Lord. Like the four blind men, everyone is sure *they are right* as they cling to their precious perspective. Church history confirms that most denominations originated with a specific emphasis on one scripture or dominant truth.

Is it possible that we are holding so tightly to our favorite doctrine that we have let go of the glorious gospel? Have we replaced the core message of Christianity with religious concepts, doctrines, and mystical mantras? Have you read a list of contemporary Christendom's teaching titles lately? Here is a sampling:

+ Creation vs. Evolutionism

+ Influencing Your Community

+ The Reality of Angels

+ Leadership Principles

+ Social Justice

+ Muslim Misconceptions

+ The Feasts of Israel

+ How to Walk by Faith

+ Breaking Demon Powers

We have many messages in the church today, each of them important. The titles listed above came from my personal library. Despite the richness of our respective teachings, though, we must remain cautious, remembering not to neglect or overlook *the* message: Jesus. We must focus on who He is and what He did. Now is the time to simplify the message of Christ. Before your relatives and coworkers become bogged down in a plethora of dos and don'ts some try to attach to Christianity, guide them to pray this one-sentence prayer, "Lord, unveil Jesus to me today."

Kerplunked in Colorado

Back in 1981, on a visit to a vibrant church in Loveland, Colorado, the Spirit spoke to me one day as I walked out of my hotel. Though a still, small voice, it thundered as if I had an invisible megaphone in my ear: "I am depositing in you the giftings of a teacher. I will teach you how to teach." Then a tangible noise sounded from within, just like a quarter that goes "kerplunk" in a vending machine. Sometimes when God speaks, it seems that time stands still, stirring an inward gasp from the holiness of the moment. This is what the psalmist meant when he said to "deep calls unto deep" (Ps. 42:7).

"Lord, I've been ministering Your Word for seven years. What do you mean about 'teaching me to teach'?" I asked.

While He did not answer immediately, six years later He continued that Colorado conversation. Six years! He simply picked up where He had left off, knowing I would recognize the conclusion of His message: "Teach Jesus. Teach who He is and what He has done. Teach Jesus." Once again I sensed that internal reverberation that sometimes accompanies His voice. It was a defining moment in my ministry, and it represented a foundational philosophy for Discovery Camps.

It is a foundation based on Scripture. After forty years as a Bible student, with more than twenty of those years functioning as a Bible school president, I feel qualified to summarize the Bible. Here's the condensed version of the central messages in three easy sentences:

The entire Old Testament: "The Messiah is coming."

The Gospels: "The Messiah has come."

The Revelation to John: "He's coming again."

To further summarize the entire Bible in one word: Jesus. Each of its sixty-six books contains a splendid portrait of our Lord. The purpose of the written Word is to point people to the Living Word. The following list of Christ's name from each book of the Bible comes from the late Oral Roberts, one of my heroes in the faith.

OLD TESTAMENT

Genesis: *Seed of Woman*

Exodus: *The Passover Lamb*

Leviticus: *High Priest*

Numbers: *Pillar of Cloud by Day; Fire by Night*

Deuteronomy: *Prophet Like Unto Moses*

Joshua: *Captain of Our Salvation*

Judges: *Faithful Judge and Lawgiver*

Ruth: *Kinsman Redeemer*

First and Second Samuel: *Trusted Prophet*

First and Second Kings: *Reigning King*

First and Second Chronicles: *Reigning King*

Ezra: *Faithful Scribe*

Nehemiah: *Restorer of the Brokenhearted*

Esther: *Faithful Mordecai*

Job: *Ever-Living Redeemer*

Psalms: *Good Shepherd*

Proverbs: *Wisdom*

Ecclesiastes: *Wisdom*

Song of Solomon: *Lover and Bridegroom*

Isaiah: *Prince of Peace*

Jeremiah: *Branch of Righteousness*

Lamentations: *Weeping Prophet*

Ezekiel: *Wonderful Four-Face Man*

Daniel: *Fourth Man in the Furnace*

Hosea: *Faithful Husband*

Joel: *Baptizer in the Holy Ghost*

Amos: *Burden Bearer*

Obadiah: *Savior*

Jonah: First *Foreign Missionary*

Micah: *Messenger With Beautiful Feet*

Nahum: *Avenger of God's Elect*

Habakkuk: *Fiery Evangelist*

Zephaniah: *Mighty to Save*

Haggai: *Restorer of My Heritage*

Zechariah: *Cleansing Fountain*

Malachi: *Son of Righteousness With Healing in His Wings*

NEW TESTAMENT

Matthew: *Messiah*

Mark: *Miracle Worker*

Luke: *Son of Man*

John: *Son of God*

Acts: *Baptizer in the Holy Ghost*

Romans: *Justifier*

First and Second Corinthians: *Sanctifier*

Galatians: *Redeemer From the Curse of the Law*

Ephesians: *Christ of Unsearchable Riches*

Philippians: *Provider*

Colossians: *Fullness of the Godhead*

First and Second Thessalonians: *Soon and Coming King*

First and Second Timothy: *Mediator Between God and Man*

Titus: *Faithful Pastor*

Philemon: *Friend Who Sticks Closer Than a Brother*

Hebrews: *Blood of the New Covenant, Lasting Forever*

James: *Great Physician*

First and Second Peter: *Chief Shepherd*

First, Second, and Third John: *Love*

Jude: *Returning Lord With 10,000 Angels*

Revelation: *King of Kings and Lord of Lords*[1]

Tommy with John Avanzini and John Osteen

Jesus IS the Message

Paul wrote to the church of Colossians about Christ, saying that "He is the head of the body, the church, who is the beginning, the first-born from the dead, that in all things He may have the preeminence" (Col. 1:18). The centrality of Jesus should undergird every sermon and Bible study. I have heard masterful orators deliver impressive sermons yet never once mention the Word Himself. As Jesus told the Pharisees, "You search the Scriptures, for in them you think you have eternal life; and these are they which testify of Me. But you are not willing to come to Me that you may have life" (John 5:39–40). Why would any pastor or teacher instruct others about the tabernacle without explaining that Jesus is our High Priest?

I listened once to a highly respected scholar teach on the seed of Abraham. He wound through a maze of Jewish genealogy, with a plethora of "so-and-so begat so-and-sos." After forty minutes of emphasizing that God allotted special blessings to His favorite people, he closed with a solemn prayer. Ugh! I wanted to scream, "Dr. Scholar, won't you use your amazing intellect to point these dear people to Jesus?" Their lives could have been revolutionized had he just added one sentence: "Through Jesus Christ you became the seed

of Abraham and a candidate for all the blessings I have explained."
The Bible contains more than two hundred titles of Jesus.[2] Each one
reveals a flash of His magnificent Person.

Does your message exalt Jesus? Heal broken lives? It matters
not whether your platform is a prestigious pulpit, a mission field,
or your kitchen table with neighborhood kids scattered around it.
Train yourself to ask these questions while developing your message:
Does this point people to Jesus? Which of the sixty-six pictures of
Jesus does it exalt? I suggest reading the Bible with the above list of
Jesus's titles in your lap. As you read some scriptures, match them
to one of those names. Then stop and praise *that* picture of Jesus.
It will bring the different facets of His personality to the forefront.
The more you know Him, the more you will love Him.

As you prepare your Bible studies or sermons, give each a sub-
title to honor Jesus. For example, instead of just teaching on "How
to Recognize God's Voice," add to the outline a point about "Jesus,
the Good Shepherd." Instead of just titling a series "Moses and the
Red Sea," consider adding "Jesus, Our Redeemer." Even Jesus gave
us an evangelistic tip when He said, "And I, if I am lifted up from
the earth, will draw all peoples to Myself" (John 12:32). Lift Him
up, not your opinions, jokes, or pet peeves. Forget the soapboxes
and focus on Jesus, the Desire of the Nations, the Bread of Life, the
Friend of Sinners, and the Soon-Coming King.

KEEP THE MESSAGE SIMPLE

God bless our Baptist friends who have mastered the salvation message of Jesus Christ. No wonder they get so many people born again.
I learned "Salvation's A-B-Cs" from them. God bless our Assemblies
of God friends too, who taught us the strength of hosting a theme
service. If you remain teachable, you will discover that all denominations have something unique to teach us. What would happen
if we could combine the Baptists' emphasis on salvation with the

freedom of charismatics while mixing in the reverence of Catholics and the structure of Methodists? Remember, the only people in heaven will be blood-bought believers. No labels needed.

We call our opening-night Miracle Rally at Discovery Camp "Say *Yes* to Jesus Night." To share the gospel, we created huge PowerPoint slides to allow campers to recite out loud:

"Salvation is as easy as A-B-C:

"A = Admit you are a sinner.

"B = Believe that Jesus died for your sins.

"C = Confess that Jesus Christ is your Savior."

The gospel is quite simple: Jesus loves me, this I know. And, Jesus knows me, this I love. There is life-changing power in the message that Jesus died, was buried, rose again, and ascended to heaven. Avoid saying only that Jesus was born to die, since such a statement neglects His resurrection and ascension. That is preaching a "cross" religion instead of a "throne" religion. I often grimace over the term "full gospel" because it implies some of my dearest friends in ministry are preaching a half gospel. On the other hand, if you insist on singing "Near the Cross," you're majoring on Jesus, our sin substitute, and neglecting Jesus, our High Priest. Yes, He died, but He is alive and functioning as our intercessor, High Priest, and mediator of the covenant. Let's enlarge our hearts and embrace *all* of the person of Jesus.

Tommy and I learned how to preach the true gospel from a mentor and special friend, Dr. T. L. Osborn. A pioneer of mass-miracle evangelism of unparalleled proportions, he and his wife, Daisy, preached open-air meetings to multiple millions in over ninety nations.[3] I challenge you to study any of this vibrant octogenarian's materials diligently; Jesus will step out of the pages of your Bible. He has summarized the gospel of Jesus Christ into eight words:

God's creation

Satan's deception

Christ's substitution

Man's restoration

You can teach this to everyone, and they can quickly become soul winners. It is as easy as A-B-C.

Missionary statesman T. L. Osborn with the lovely Dodie Osteen

A MOO-VING EXPERIENCE

During our first few years—before we saw thousands coming every summer—we took campers on hayrides that allowed them to enjoy our back property adjoining the Colorado River. Since most visitors had not grown up camping under the stars or roasting marshmallows over a campfire, this was quite a treat. One night as about four hundred teens gathered in the dark around a rustic amphitheatre for praise and a short message, a leader named Kenny said, "Bow your heads, young people. This is the most important moment of your entire camp visit. If you want to accept Jesus Christ as your personal Lord and Savior, since it's too dark to see your hand, simply say, 'Jesus, save me.'"

No response followed.

"Don't be embarrassed," Kenny added after an awkward silence. "I sense the Lord wants me to encourage you to say yes to Jesus right now. Who will say yes to Jesus right now?"

"Moo-ooo!" bellowed out a neighbor's cow with a silence-sapping sound that could have raised the dead. I heard a giggle. Then roars of laughter exploded. We all rejoiced that Mr. Grimes's cow got "saved" at Discovery Camp.

An amusing story, but it makes a serious point: it is imperative to present the gospel accurately. Many aren't serving the Lord today because a messenger portrayed only one aspect of God's character or misrepresented Him altogether. As a tragic result, people today have many misconceptions about God. Some think of Him as a policeman, lingering in the shadows to catch them speeding. Others look at Him as a heavenly Santa Claus who gives gifts to only good little girls and boys. Another popular misconception of God is that He is like a divine vending machine, where you can put in a prayer and pull out a Porsche or put in a scripture and pull out a spouse. The truth of the matter—God is a Father, not a grandfather. If you need to know the difference, just consider which one spoils your darlings and then sends them back home.

THE POWER OF A THEME

When it comes to gospel presentations, I believe themes make a great idea. The purpose of a theme is to provide repetitive opportunities to present the message of Christ. Themes are effective because few people grasp a truth the first time they hear it. This explains the statement that our TBI students hear frequently: "Repetition is the best teacher." Psychologists teach that the comprehension factor for the average person's intellect is three complete readings.

Before *branding* became a buzzword in marketing circles, Discovery Camp used themes to introduce different portraits of

Jesus, such as "A Focal Point" or "The Blessed Bull's-Eye." We make a big deal of announcing our summer theme. Friends often ask how we select them; our approach has varied throughout the years. Some were prophetic words birthed during prayer. We selected others while eating chips and salsa with our staff or in ski clothes on family vacations. I believe that themes are so powerful that we could select "Scooby-Doo" and watch the Holy Spirit somehow make it anointed. Themes can be reinforced by décor, music, videos, testimonies, costumes, banners, or outlines, but they must point to Jesus. As I've said, Jesus *is* the message.

Leaders might be interested in how the power of a theme assists our presentation of the gospel's miracle message. This prototype works in ladies' outreaches, prison ministries, home meetings, or mass gatherings. We condense our summer themes into a one-sentence summary, known to our ministry team as an OSS, which stands for one-sentence summary. It serves as the bull's-eye in the target. Every skit, testimony, video, or special song should ideally hit that target from different angles, thereby reaching different types of ages and personalities.

When campers give their testimonies, they always refer to the summer by the theme, not the year: "I gave my life to Jesus at 'Dream Big' and then decided to attend TBI at 'Born for Greatness!'" This is why we always have a theme banner, a theme song, and a theme T-shirt. This is in keeping with the fact that God's Word has a theme: JESUS.

THE MESSAGE AND ITS MESSENGERS

Like sprinkles on a cupcake, different personalities add a fun flavor to God's family. Some who minister are soft-spoken. Some are seminar-oriented. Others are what I call "screamers." We should mature to the level that we can receive anything from anyone, as long as they preach the genuine, biblically based gospel. While Tommy and I have differing styles, we have learned to celebrate our differences. For the first ten years of Discovery Camp I led the morning sessions, which emphasized the importance of the Word. Tommy led the evening rallies, which focused on the altar of the Lord.

We explained to guests that "filling up your head" and "filling up your heart" are needed, and that the written Word is a map that leads you to the Living Word. This occurred quite naturally because I am an early bird and Tommy is more of a night owl. These twice-daily rallies are as different as apples and oranges. We came by this quite naturally, as I lean toward teaching and Tommy leans toward exploding.

Truthfully Tommy has never fit very well into my neatly contained themes or my organized way of doing things. My morning sessions were exactly seventy-five minutes, hitting that trophied theme repetitively (there's that word again) through songs, skits, sermonettes, and testimonies. I love my themes! Not Tommy. He embraces one theme: explode. For more than thirty years I have marveled at, and revered, the anointing on his life. Others can tell you how humorous it is to see Mrs. Day-Themer and Mr. Night-Exploder blend for the glory of God.

For the first twelve years of our camps Tommy ministered at each night's Miracle Rally. Much to my chagrin they contained no structure whatsoever. Often he would preach first and then open up the altars. However, he might also stroll into these rallies and say, "Lift your hands," and the power of God would fall. No "hello" or "I'm glad to be with you." TBI alumni working with us learned to brace for the impact of these moves of God. To some it probably looked like mass chaos, with teens pushing their way to the altar to be delivered of drugs and bodies crumbling to the floor under the power of the Spirit.

Tommy would preach all the way through these moves, sometimes to hundreds listening and laughing at his stories, and sometimes directly to one camper. Then he would pause and I would think, "Thank God, he's realizing how late it is," only to watch him look in a particular direction and smile, "Hey, what are you waiting for? You know that Jesus has called you into full-time ministry." Such a remark would set off a stampede of more campers to the altar, and another wave of God's glory would roll over the crowd.

In such times I could imagine the prophet Joel leaning over the balcony of heaven, shouting, "Go, Tommy, go! That's exactly what I saw in my vision. The Spirit is being poured out upon your sons and daughters." Wave after wave, hour after hour, night after night, and year after year Tommy has exploded with the love, joy, and power of God. By our third summer I gave up trying to fit him into our neat little camp themes. Clearly his is "Explode," and he explodes quite well.

Now it's not that I didn't want him to explode. I just wanted the explosions to be orderly. It boggled my organized, peanut brain that he didn't seem to notice or care that the ministry lines of campers were crooked, Kleenex tissues were not available for sobbing youth, nor were men available to catch hundreds of campers falling under the power of God. I would often stick Post-it notes on the pulpit saying, "Reminder: Camp theme is 'Day of Choices,'" but it would get blown off by the winds of God, along with my service schedule.

Our marriage became sweeter when I recognized Tommy's theme focused solely on Jesus. I wanted to give the campers a picture of Jesus, as you would a slice of pie. Not my husband. He gives campers the whole enchilada. His unique anointing invites people to experience the multifaceted person of Christ. Sometimes it is a glimpse of His mercy or a peek into His purpose or often the delivering power of His presence. The moral of the story, folks, is that when it comes to the preaching of the gospel, celebrate anyone and any style or, as the saying goes, we ought to be smart enough to eat the fish and spit out the bones.

WHAT YOU PREACH IS WHAT YOU GET

Do you know why our Baptist friends get so many people saved while the prophetic "camps" have so many dreams and visions? Or why Word of Faith people see so many financial breakthroughs and apostolics so many healings? The answer, which Tommy and I have observed for decades, is simple: they lift up that specific picture of the Lord Jesus and *what you preach is what you get*. The Baptists have a dynamic salvation message, spotlighting the cross of Calvary and the shed blood of Jesus, and thousands get born again. Healing revivals swept through our nation in the 1940s and 1950s because Oral Roberts and others introduced people to Jesus the Healer. When you preach about Jesus the Deliverer, people get set free.

Regardless of your style or topic, let me encourage anyone who ministers publicly to consider these three suggestions:

1. Pray until you get the mind of the Lord. Stay on foundational Bible topics that reveal Jesus, such as who He is, what He did, and what He is doing today.

2. Diligently study. I groan when a minister opens with: "I'd just like to share some things on my heart." That indicates they didn't have the discipline to fill their head. Write out your outline or—even more impressive—type out your entire message. I call it "planned but not canned." The Spirit can lead your thoughts on Tuesday afternoon as easily as on Sunday morning. Some of our "shoot off the hip share from our heart" ministry is really a lack of disciplined study. (Whew! I feel better just saying that.)

3. Learn some basics in public speaking. When I was a nursing student back in the 1970s, a pastor once

asked me if I had ever taken homiletics. Not knowing that homiletics was a course on skillful preaching, I responded, "No sir, I've been healthy all of my life." The basics of having one nail (topic) and three chances (points) to drive it in is a good start. Even professional speakers and wise preachers realize their best speeches have one primary thought that they express many different ways.

FAMOUS SERMONS

Christian historians are prone to list Jonathan Edwards' "Sinners in the Hands of an Angry God" or John Wesley's "The Almost Christian" as their favorite sermons. However, my all-time favorite was not delivered but demonstrated by Tommy at Discovery Camp in 1999. Everyone attending that night would unanimously concur. The Spirit-led spontaneity embedded a visual for us all that marked our lives eternally.

Here is what happened. Tommy stands six feet, three inches tall, and he has dancing blue eyes that accent his joy. An adult visitor once remarked, "Tommy's as much fun to watch as he is listen to." During Tommy's legendary Miracle Rallies, the gifts of the Spirit would operate, accompanied by amazing impartations and demonstrations. Always. Were it not for his keen sense of humor, I'm sure he would have scared most campers and intimidated other leaders (ask anyone who knows him). He has some of the most irreverent ways to host God's presence and enjoy His people. If I didn't know him personally—his sterling character and his long-lasting fruit—even I might raise an eyebrow.

One habit he developed during our lengthy praise-a-thons was drinking from his glass of water and randomly throwing the rest into the crowd. Imagine one thousand campers at the altar jumping and praising Jesus, only to get splashed in the face. Some thought it was "holy water," but most people recognized Tommy's spirit of mischief. As the nature of pranks goes, one glass evolved into several. At some camps several buckets of water got tossed twenty feet into screaming-for-Jesus teenagers. They loved it. It was just clean, wholesome fun and quite a stark contrast to some of their rigid, legalistic churches. (By the way, until you've operated a camp for twenty-five years, please don't send me any mean letters about this.)

Then it happened. A spunky camper somehow found a glass of water, climbed up the three marble steps of the Ambassador's Hall stage, and threw the water right into Tommy's face! How presumptuous. The staff gasped. The music stopped. Time stood still. Everyone was stunned that this scrawny kid would do this. Two of our staffers grabbed the kid, waiting on instructions from Tommy. Planning to demonstrate sweet revenge, Tommy brought him farther onto the stage. In a spirit of wholesome fun he taunted and teased him with a Texas-size bucket of water over his head. Campers cheered Tommy on as if he was a Roman gladiator.

Just then Tommy had an inspired idea how to turn that prank into an altar call. Grinning spontaneously at the prankster, he said, "I love you. Now step aside. I'll take that bucket of water for you." He then stepped directly under it and instructed his staff to pour it on him. After they were convinced he really meant it, POUR they did. Tommy was as drenched as if he had jumped in the swimming pool. After the huge *gasp!* that followed, Tommy said, "This is a simple picture of the love that Jesus Christ had for you on a cross called Calvary. I took the bucket of water that this boy deserved. But Jesus went to a cross that you deserved. I took his punishment so this camper could go free. But Jesus took your sin so you could go free. What a Savior! If you'll run to His love right now, you can also be released from the punishment of your sin and live with Him forever." Hundreds received Jesus as their Savior that night, including that mischievous kid.

WHAT'S YOUR LIFE MESSAGE?

Whether behind a pulpit, a computer, or on the sports field, we are all preaching messages. What is your life's message? You are a steward of this miracle message too and are especially influential over your loved ones. What are your unspoken actions saying? Is regular church attendance a priority? Do your children see you reading your Bible? Do they hear you groan about tithing? Do they see you hide your beer when church friends come over? To those curious little eyes watching you, the latter two examples translate into hypocrisy big-time. You are sending messages that can quickly cause your Christian legacy to crumble. As St. Francis of Assisi said, "Preach the gospel at all times and when necessary use words."[4] Those words are as relevant today as when he wrote them in 1215. You might be the only Bible that some people read.

I would like to remind parents about two things concerning the message they are sending to their children. First, pay particular attention to what you say to others while your child is in the room. Although he may seem focused on that video game, your child hears when you apologize for his dirty shirt and shaggy hair. That trans-lates to him that he isn't good enough and embarrasses his mother. Doesn't that just make you want to go find the nearest kid and hug him? When our children were playing in the room, I intentionally shared a story about an area of character growth. "Peter is getting so good about sharing his new Nerf gun with Andrew," I would say to our guests, knowing in my heart that only happened once compared to three temper tantrums. Yet I sent the message: "Good choices make Mama proud of me."

Secondly, to parents with teenagers in your home, be careful to honor people in authority. A frequent comment among our church-bred Bible students concerns references to the hypocrisy they see at home. If you expect them to respect authority, they need to see you respect your employer. If you expect them to enjoy church, that means you must never serve Roast Pastor or Drench the Deacon for Sunday dinner.

Do You Qualify
to Share the Gospel?

"I-I-I'm n-n-not too g-g-good at t-t-talking in front of p-p-people," stuttered one of our sons in the Lord, "b-b-but I didn't c-c-come today to impress, b-b-but to impart." For the next twenty minutes the good news of the gospel poured out of his heart and radically rearranged lives. Our Discovery Camp ministry teams are not polished pulpiteers but simply young Bible Institute alumni who have a genuine call upon their lives to minister. Some calmly stand in one spot like a statue, while others pace the stage like a lion about to pounce. There is nothing more effective than a pure, authentic testimony of Jesus's love that has turned someone inside out. Quite often I have these speakers write out three-point sermons until they are secure enough to create their own. Until they give me a strong OSS, I send them back to their dorm room to rework their message. Yes, I'm strict, but churches are trusting us to provide quality ministry, and young ministers need to learn to honor the pulpit.

Toss out any stereotype of how you need to look or act to minister to young people (or any age, for that matter). Neither Tommy nor I are "cool" by any stretch of the imagination—not even in our younger years. Still, we have learned that a young teen who has just admitted to a secret abortion doesn't need someone "cool"; she needs Christ's unconditional love. God is not looking for ability but availability. My concept of cool now includes those retired, overweight, not-so-cool adults who bring young people from their church to camp. Despite their fanny packs, they are emotionally stable and relaxed enough to tolerate the stupidity that goes with kids. Their nonverbal message is louder than the most impressive oratory. Their listening ears and loving arms are as a balm of Gilead. We even have grandparents who serve as camp chaperones and sleep on the top bunk. Don't allow age or lack of coolness to disqualify you from ministry. When people are thirsty, they don't care if a cold drink is served in Waterford crystal or a Dixie cup. Give yourself away. That's cool.

The Gospel Releases Miracles

The gospel is a miracle message, so if you are preaching it accurately, you will always see miracles. Learn to live with a spirit of expectancy. When I step onto the Discovery Camp stage, I am whispering, "Lord Jesus, what do You want to do today?" One evening He replied, "There are four girls present who have been diagnosed with scoliosis. Let's heal them tonight." Wasn't the way He worded it interesting? I announced, "Jesus is our Healer, and if you have curvature of the spine, please come forward so He can heal you." Exactly four girls between the ages of twelve and twenty came forward, and their spines were supernaturally healed. Two did backbends on the stage as the crowd cheered.

In 1989 a fifteen-year-old and some of his "homies" were sitting on the back row of a Discovery Youth Camp. They planned to trash the facilities after the service, but Jesus interrupted their plans. "Young man on the back row," boomed Tommy's voice, his finger pointing directly at Frank. "You have your plans, but God has a plan too. Trust Him tonight. He's calling you to preach His gospel." The young man surrendered that night to God's call and today is a pastor in Arkansas.

After you preach the Living Word, give Him time to move among His people. Open your sermons with, "After I teach the Word of God, you can expect a miracle of any kind, because Mark 16:20 says that 'they went out and preached everywhere, the Lord working with them and confirming the word through the accompanying signs.'" God says amen through miracles. Don't just preach the gospel—demonstrate it. We usually have fifty campers stand to represent a miracle that occurred during each of our daily Miracle Rallies. You can do the same because miracles are not the result of a personality or powerful sermon. They are the result of the gospel of Jesus Christ.

THE MIRACLE OF THE GOSPEL

Religions are man's search for God; the Gospel is God's search for man.
—E. Stanley Jones[5]

In redemption, Jesus transferred to us His nature, His anointing, His authority, His power, His name and His righteousness. He sat down, so we could stand up!
—T. L. Osborn[6]

For every text in Scripture, there is a road to the metropolis of the Scriptures, that is Christ.
—Charles Spurgeon[7]

Preach the gospel at all times and when necessary use words.
—Francis of Assisi

The Judge who pronounced you guilty also paid your fine.
—Tony Evans[8]

Be sincere. Be brief. Be seated.
—Franklin D. Roosevelt

CHAPTER 6

God Hasn't Lost His Recipe for Manna

ॐ **Life Question:** If God owns it all, why am I lacking?

ॐ **Miracle Moment:** The miracle of abundance

ॐ **Life Lesson:** Where God guides, He provides.

AFTER DECADES OF DEPENDING ON GOD, I CAN SAFELY SAY that it is amazing what He can do all by Himself! Every leader in ministry has experienced balancing the endless demand for finances with his or her desperate desire to do more for God. Early in our walk together at Discovery Camp Tommy and I made a covenant with each other to obey God wholeheartedly, never merchandise the anointing, and never, never, never develop sticky fingers. To assure that we could put the ministry on solid financial footing, Tommy refused to receive a salary for the first five years. I believe much of the supernatural provision in our lives is a direct result of that covenant. As we strive to do God's bidding, He has been faithful to exceed our greatest expectations.

When we started, a retired accountant asked us how we planned to pay for everything, such as six thousand dollars in monthly land payments, food for thousands of campers, and staff salaries. I remember thinking, "What a dumb question. Doesn't he know that God provides where He guides?"

To give you some quick background, for several years Tommy

and I had led successful youth ministries, first separately and then as a couple. When we married, it represented the grand climax to our respective youth ministers' networks. Brimming with optimism as we set out on our camp venture, we mailed out newsletters to two thousand friends and ministry contacts, inviting them to support us for five dollars per month. Initially I questioned Tommy: "Only five dollars? Why not suggest ten? Or perhaps twenty-five."

"No, Rachel," he responded. "Only five dollars. They are all members of a good church, and our objective is be a 'friend to the local church.'"

Reality struck us between the eyes a month later when only forty-two people responded to our newsletter. It didn't take long to do some mental math—$5 dollars times forty-two people equaled $210. Suddenly that $6,000 land payment looked more like $60,000.

"Tommy," I whined, "what are we going to do?"

Grinning, he replied, "We're gonna get busy reaching kids for Jesus like He sent us here to do because God is faithful."

I'm not even sure how we made those first few payments, but we remained faithful and steady. I watched, amazed, as we were never late on our mortgage or other bills. Plus, Jesus would not allow us to call anyone for financial assistance. He continually reminded us: "Men are not your source."

Give Yourself Away

Tommy learned the lesson of depending on God so thoroughly that instead of sharing about our camp vision, he became consumed with serving others, lifting pastors' burdens, and acting as a genuine friend to churches. In that first year he preached in four hundred pulpits, often in two cities the same day. For a long time he packed a few young men into a burgundy Chevy Astro van with him. They would pray all the way there and praise the Lord all the way home. If I felt secure with the church's nursery, sometimes the kids and

I would go. When I did, my Monday morning phone calls to our finance department went something like this:

Julia: "Good morning! Did Brother Tommy have a great trip?"

Me: "Oh yes! It was jam-packed."

Julia: "Will you be sending me the honorarium before noon?"

Me: "Oh. He gave it back to the pastor."

Julia: "Why????"

Me: "They were in the middle of a building campaign."

Julia: "So are we. Well, did he sell a lot of tapes?"

Me: "Uhhhh, we didn't sell any tapes, Julia. We threw them into the congregation like Frisbees. It was a blast."

Julia: "Y'all gave away *a-l-l-l-l* the tapes?"

Me: "Yes, but we connected with so many wonderful people."

Julia: "Great. Well, at least he'll be preaching again this Wednesday."

Me: "Hey, one more thing. There's a list coming your way with the names and shoe sizes of the staff children. Tommy wants to bless them with back-to-school shoes."

Eventually Tommy earned his pilot's license and bought a plane. He always purchased the fuel so he wouldn't be a burden to the host church (and he later gave that plane away). Tommy is one amazing man who has indeed taught us all the meaning of the saying "We are blessed to be a blessing." Hundreds of pastors from his road ministry greatly respected him for it.

SURRENDER RELEASES SURPLUS

God revealed Himself to Abram (whom He renamed Abraham) first as Jehovah Elyon, the Most High God, and then as El Shaddai, God Almighty. Had Abram done anything to deserve those flashes of revelation? Absolutely. Both experiences were a reward for his obedience to leave a pagan world and then respectively enter into a covenant. Abraham's next encounter with Jehovah came at the top of Mount Moriah, as he prepared to sacrifice his son Isaac:

> When they arrived at the place where God had told him to go, Abraham built an altar and arranged the wood on it. Then he tied his son, Isaac, and laid him on the altar on top of the wood. And Abraham picked up the knife to kill his son as a sacrifice. At that moment the angel of the LORD called to him from heaven, "Abraham! Abraham!" "Yes," Abraham replied. "Here I am!" "Don't lay a hand on the boy!" the angel said. "Do not hurt him in any way, for now I know that you truly fear God. You have not withheld from me even your son, your only son." Then Abraham looked up and saw a ram caught by its horns in a thicket. So he took the ram and sacrificed it as a burnt offering in place of his son.
>
> —GENESIS 22:9–13, NLT

Abraham's obedience created an explosion of time-released, supernatural prosperity. God has delightful ways to keep His promises in front of us. For example, what two nouns did the Lord use to describe Abraham's posterity? Sand and stars—the very things surrounding Abraham. As the morning sun glistened upon miles of sand, Abraham heard the Lord whisper, "So shall your descendants be." At night he would flip open the tent flap and stare up to the stars and hear, "So shall your descendants be." These two promises appear in Genesis 13 and 15. God promised victorious descendants who would bless all the nations of the earth, all because Abraham obeyed Him.

I call your attention to two revelations in this story:

1. Jehovah Jireh wasn't a name for the Lord; it was the name of a place where Abraham offered his best. You

can visit that place as well. When you do, Jehovah
Jireh will shower provision on you as well.

2. Notice that supernatural provision followed total surrender. Some people want Abraham's blessings, but
they want to hold on to their "Isaacs." When you surrender your best, the Lord releases His best.

One time I observed the sad consequences of refusing to surrender everything to God. As I stood on the platform of a Discovery
Camp, I felt my eyes drawn to an unusually beautiful blonde girl
who looked like she was about sixteen years old. I would call her
a "Barbie-Doll-Cutie-Pa-Tootie." As she stood at the altar, I marveled at her love for Jesus—her hands straight in the air and her face
appearing lost in worship as she sang the old hymn "I Surrender
All." To be so young, so beautiful, and so passionate for Jesus! I was
thoroughly impressed until my Holy Trainer whispered, "Would
you like to see what her heart is singing?" Inwardly I nodded. Next
I heard an X-ray version as her heart sang:

"I surrender everything but my boyfriend.
I surrender everything but my boyfriend."

In the spirit realm I saw her raised hands become fists defying
His supremacy over her life. Ugh. Suddenly she became the ugliest
camper at the altar. I prayed that she would quickly learn that God
can't bless half-hearted worship, and that her Ken was not created
to be her god. Conditional surrender closes heaven's windows.

DARE TO BE DEBT FREE

In January of 1992 faith rose up in our hearts to pay off the mortgage on the camp property. Tommy led our staff in a strong confession of faith: "By December thirty-first this ministry will be

debt free." We confessed this constantly, despite our bills dramatically increasing each month. By the way, miracles don't happen just because you repeat something over and over like a parrot. You need to understand that the Holy Spirit deposits in your heart the faith to believe for something. He makes suggestions that you can accept or reject. If you choose to agree with God and mix your confession with faith, you will receive the manifestation. I'm not referring to a selfish-oriented "blab it and grab it" type claim but a genuine faith promise that advances the kingdom of God. When God is the initiator, He is inviting you to be a part of a miracle.

Dear Tommy felt financial burdens falling on his shoulders that year. The costs of operating a 553-acre campus requiring ongoing maintenance of land and vehicles, staff housing, insurance, and food costs seemed to be regularly escalating. We rejoiced if the monthly electric bill stayed under $20,000, while Tommy said things like, "Lord, if You help me pay this camp off, I'll give away free camps to hurting kids." Keep in mind, no megachurch or rich men's committee underwrote us, just faithful pastors, partners, and friends who obeyed His voice. We had numerous "five-dollar grandmas" who accepted the call to intercede. Great will be their reward in heaven.

To any of you working for the Lord, let me give you a tip. You have to come to the place where you declare confidently, "Man is not my source, the mail is not my source, and events are not my source. God is my source." We spent that entire year standing on His promise to be debt free by the end of the year. On December 24 I looked at the calendar and wondered why God seems to take such pleasure in last-minute miracles! Friends, don't let go of your promise in your eleventh hour. God is faithful. Although it seems today the world goes on vacation the week of Christmas, by December 26 we had the funds in the bank. However, we still needed some legal paperwork to be completed. Our confession remained strong because we knew that "He who promised is faithful" (Heb. 10:23).

As I said earlier, sometimes you are waiting on the Lord when He is actually waiting for you. Sometimes if the door doesn't open, you have to kick it down. Such was the case for our debt-free miracle. Tommy drove three hundred miles to collect the necessary paperwork and then drove another two hundred miles to finalize everything. Although some banks weren't open because of the Christmas holidays, and some doors slammed in our face, we never wavered in our confession of faith. On December 29, with a check in hand for $139,604.35, we raced to the title company. Against all odds, and to the glory of God, we paid off the 553 acres of Country Camp on the last business day of the year.

TOMMY KEPT HIS VOW

In gratitude for God's goodness and remembering Tommy's vow, the next year we committed to give free camps to two thousand underprivileged kids. We covered their registration and food and underwrote the four-hundred-dollar fee for a rental bus to bring them here. Some came from orphanages or lived on the streets with their homeless mothers. We saw no Scooby-Doo sleeping bags or designer jeans at those camps. One child's lunch plate shook as he marveled, "I've never seen so much food on one plate!" Ninety-nine percent of the children and adult chaperones received Jesus as their personal Savior.

At the conclusion of one of these camps the head count revealed a missing child. Our amazing trained staff covered their zones methodically and finally found a small eight-year-old boy hiding in a tree. He reluctantly came down, but then screamed, "Please don't send me home. My father b-e-a-t-s me." While we had to send him home, we explained that Jesus would be his protector.

More than twenty years later we have remained true to our vow.

More than twenty-five thousand children from impoverished backgrounds have enjoyed free camps, and most of them have decided to follow Christ. So have many of their chaperones. It seems that giving camps to these poor children opened the windows of heaven and released a series of supernatural provisions. Solomon addressed this principle twice in Proverbs: "He who has pity on the poor lends to the LORD, and He will pay back what he has given" (Prov. 19:17), and "He who gives to the poor will not lack" (Prov. 28:27).

SUPERNATURAL PROPERTY

Tommy had just completed an outstanding sermon series titled "Seizing Your God-Given Opportunities" when a good friend called to alert us to a feed store in the process of being dismantled in Uvalde, Texas. Even at a super-low price, buying iron from the dismantled building sounded like a hassle, yet he felt an inner witness to pursue it. When the Scriptures don't speak specifically about a subject, you can always trust your inner witness. I call it "my knower" because it helps me know that I know. After the iron was delivered to the camp, we learned it was worth double the amount we paid. Another case of supernatural provision! We used it to build TBI classrooms.

We saw the same come true with our camp road, which started out as 1,800 feet of dirt base. In Texas we enjoy what the locals call "gully washers," which are relentless, torrential rainstorms. For nine years we lived regularly with mud, mud, and more mud. Campers routinely tracked mud into the dorms and chapel. Our guests' vehicles frequently got mired in the muck. We used to joke that in heaven our shoes wouldn't be muddy. Although we stayed focused on our God-given mandate to serve local churches and reach young people for Christ, sometimes the mud exasperated our patience.

Still, like Paul, we also declared, "I know how to be abased, and I know how to abound" (Phil. 4:12). Finally faith rose up in our heart to spread an oil cap over the road. We sent out a letter to our precious pastors, partners, and friends and issued a strong appeal in our monthly magazine *Signs and Wonders Today*. We were surprised that our partners didn't embrace this need immediately. But after many months of standing in faith, a man called for Tommy while he was ministering in Odessa, Texas, at one of our wonderful partner churches. The man told Tommy that while he was praying that morning, the Lord told him that he was to cover the expenses of a camp project we were working on.

Since we didn't know this man personally, Tommy questioned him further.

"Praise the Lord, brother," he said. "You must have experienced our muddy road firsthand."

"No, I haven't been there for years," the caller replied.

"Oh, I see. Well, you must have received our partner letter asking for help."

"No, Tommy, I was in prayer and the Lord Jesus assigned me to cover the expenses of a camp project."

In one last attempt to figure it all out, Tommy asked, "Perhaps you read about this need in our magazine?" (He wasn't a doubting Thomas, just curious.)

Somewhat aggravated, the man responded, "No, Tommy, I don't receive the magazine. I told you that I was in prayer this morning and the Lord Jesus told me to cover the expenses of a camp project. Now tell me what you need, and I'll put it in the mail."

Thank God Tommy had the sense to quit probing before the man got angry and changed his mind. Sometimes trying to figure out God's leading can mess up a miracle. One week later our financial secretary called Tommy and said, "Sir, I have good news. The funds have arrived!" Today campers, pastors, partners, and friends drive through a handsome array of twenty American flags and flowers and enter our campus via a lovely, paid-for, one-and-a-half-mile-long-paved road. God has good people every-where who are quick to obey the nudges of the Holy Spirit and help ministries like yours and ours. To this day I don't know the name of that kind man, but his offering of twelve thousand dollars has blessed thousands of our guests. Thank God for an end to the mud!

Yet another miracle story of our development involves the building of a sixteen-room, hotel-style building in 1996 to serve as quarters where pastors and leaders could refresh. Since God had called us to be a "friend to the local church," we affectionately named it Shepherd's Inn. Just days away from its grand opening, though, we still desperately needed funds and workers. At a men's advance, two wonderful members of our board of regents presented us with an offering of $43,000 for its completion. It was the only time in my fifty-plus years that I remember being truly speechless. Still scrambling to have the inn open by our "Leadership Summit '97," we then saw a sweet-natured couple appear to offer to paint the interior. No one knew who they were, but with the clock ticking, we put them to work. They did an excellent job, and we have never seen them again. We even wondered if we had "unwittingly entertained angels" (Heb. 13:2).

Four Eighteen-Wheeler Miracles

Back in the early 1990s Tommy often preached about the bigness of God. He liked to roar out in faith, "Psalm 68:19 says, 'Blessed be the Lord, who daily loads us with benefits.' Why, if you just dare to believe for big things, God will bring your blessing on an eighteen-wheeler."

Over the next decade we had four unscheduled eighteen-wheelers arrive with our "daily load."

Eighteen-wheeler #1: Candy

One day when our helper Jennifer answered the Bible Institute phone line, the caller said, "I need directions to your place so I can deliver this candy." She wasn't aware of any such order, but it wasn't unusual for food to be delivered. Two hours later an eighteen-wheeler arrived, filled with nine tons of candy—which no one had ordered. Have you ever even seen how much nine tons of candy is? (That's fifty thousand dollars worth.) This was a custom-made miracle too, because the shipment contained our campers' favorite candy bars. We finally traced it back to a dear woman who had referred us to the Hershey Company, which responded by designating nineteen palettes of candy for Discovery Camp. (On a side note, we often encouraged our amazing staff after long hours in the hot Texas sun, "Your payday is coming, and you'll be eternally rewarded for your labors of love." What did we find in that order? Hundreds of PayDay candy bars. God has such a fun sense of humor!)

Eighteen-wheelers #2, #3, and #4: Furniture, grass, and mulch

An eighteen-wheeler arrived in 1994 filled with beautiful furniture that I inherited from an aunt who had no children. In 2002 another eighteen-wheeler showed up filled with grass from a partnering church. The following year another arrived with mulch from a TBI alumnus' family—twenty-two pallets of wood mulch valued at $5,300. Some people don't get too excited about grass and mulch, but since we were surrounded by 553 acres of mud, we recognized this as supernatural provision. Tommy's prophetic challenge came true.

God has supernatural provisions prepared for you as well. Tommy and I are not God's favorites, but we are careful to stay focused on what is important to Him. "Seek first the kingdom of God and His righteousness, and all these things [such as grass, mulch, candy, and furniture] shall be added to you" (Matt. 6:33).

God doesn't care if you have things, as long as things don't have you. When your priorities are His priorities, He will literally send heaven's best to assist you. This isn't about fulfilling your dream life. It's about releasing His dream into the earth.

Let me be clear: I believe God wants believers to prosper with as much as He can trust them with. God is a Father. The New Testament refers to Him as a Father no less than 245 times, including more than 100 times in the Gospel of John.[1] The issue of a believer's prosperity is not his treasures but his pleasures. There are three scriptural reasons God gives blessings:

- To establish His covenant on the earth
- So we can be a blessing to others
- So we may enjoy personal blessings as an expression of God's goodness

If you are ready to serve God wholeheartedly, whether abased or abounding, God can trust you and prosper you.

Fifty thousand dollars worth of free candy!

Who's Your Daddy?

I like to share the story about two girls who met at a camp on the East Coast. A bratty, rich girl introduced herself to the other: "Hey there. I come here every summer because my daddy owns part of this property. Do you see that speedboat on the lake? My daddy owns that boat. Do you see that mansion on the side of the mountain? My daddy stays there when he comes to visit me." Looking upward, she then exclaimed, "Oh! Do you see that airplane? That's my daddy," and waved enthusiastically, as if the passengers could actually see her.

"So, who's your daddy?" she asked in a condescending tone.

The other preteen was a good Christian girl but wasn't wealthy. In fact, her mother had sold some of her personal jewelry to cover the camp's registration fees. Feeling embarrassed and insignificant, the girl looked down at the dirt by their cabin. Suddenly she smiled and lifted her dejected head. With a twinkle in her eyes she said, "Do you see that large lake that your daddy's boat is in? My Father created that lake. And you know that mountain your daddy's cabin is on? My Father owns that mountain. As a matter of fact, do you see that big, blue sky your daddy's plane is in? My Father owns that sky."

After reading that kind of story, you might be thinking, "So if God owns it all, why am I lacking?" The quick answer is that you possibly have a wrong perspective or the wrong priorities. Perspective is everything, as shown by a recent experience Tommy and I had. On a dark county road we noticed a red, out-of-control pick-up truck approximately three hundred feet in front of us. Weaving back and forth, the driver jerked the truck back and forth and then sashayed into a circular pattern. We immediately called 911 to alert the authorities, only to discover later that the driver worked for the Texas Department of Public Safety and was testing a new type of road base. From our limited perspective he was a drunken fool. In reality, this good man was working late at night to keep our roads safe.

Perhaps you have a wrong perspective of God, believing that He wants you to barely get along. God is not like an earthly father who would say to his son, "Now, son, you know that I am a millionaire, but I don't want you to become proud, so you can have only a dollar for lunch today." No, no—a thousand times no. He is a loving father who would say something more like, "After football practice, let's go out for pizza; in fact, invite the whole team." Likewise I challenge you to renew your mind and think bigger. Spend some time in Isaiah, where it says, "Behold, the nations are as a drop in a bucket, and are counted as the small dust on the scales; look, He lifts up the isles as a very little thing" (Isa. 40:15). One drop. Ponder that when your faucet drips tonight. Let one drop fall on a plate and stare at it. In God's mind that drop represents 196 nations of the earth. As an old Hebrew would say, "*Selah*" (stop and listen). You can tap into the invisible, unlimited resources of heaven by meditating on His greatness.

Many people live from problem to problem and bill to bill, but you can climb out of that rut through generosity. Our debt to God is made payable to man. We have some friends who set a personal goal to tithe 90 percent of their income to God's work and live on 10 percent. It took them thirty years, but they are now retired and are some of the happiest people on earth. Their stories of constant supernatural surplus are astounding. Why wouldn't God bless them? He knows their priority is to advance His kingdom. Don't wait until you can afford to give to God's work. Start where you are. If you planned to give fifty dollars to the work of God, give fifty-three. I dare you to pray, "Lord, I will give away any extra money that I earn, find, or receive this week." Perhaps it will be a quarter under the couch or a product rebate you forgot about. Don't be surprised when it arrives, and promptly keep your vow. How big is God? As big as you will allow Him to be.

Prosperity with a purpose comes with a responsibility too. God blesses you so that you can become a blessing to your relatives, your church, your city, and the world. To achieve this mind-set, meditate on 3 John 2: "Beloved, I wish above all things that thou mayest prosper and be in health, even as thy soul prospereth" (KJV). The secret to true prosperity lies in renewing your soul, which is your mind, will, and emotions. We all have to deal with some "stinkin' thinkin'" by rejecting wrong thoughts about surplus, as if those who have an abundance must have done something wrong to get it. While that may be true sometimes, it isn't always the case, particularly when God causes His children to prosper. Accept the believer's role on the earth today—the world certainly needs more people willing to radically give to Him.

FOUR LIES THAT HINDER ABUNDANCE

There is an abundance of lies in the world that prevent people from accepting God's abundance for their lives. Here are four primary ones:

Lie #1: God wants you poor.

Why do people fight so hard to be poor? There is an old joke about the deacon who prayed for the pastor: "Lord, You keep him humble, and we'll keep him poor." How sad. Instead of craving more to lavish on yourself, imagine how—if you had more—you could do more to help others. God's covenant was to prosper His people so extravagantly that it would be a witness to the world. God takes pleasure in the prosperity of His servants (Ps. 35:27).

Lie #2: Prosperity is equivalent to monetary wealth.

Financial surplus is only one part of God's plan for abundance. Loving families, fulfilling relationships, vibrant health, and lives of purpose are included in the abundant life Jesus described in John 10:10.

Lie #3: You can't afford to tithe.

What a deceptive lie. In truth, you can't afford not to tithe. The tithe is not yours to negotiate; it is God's and it is holy. The Israelites paid their tithe as a debt, but since Jesus Christ paid our sin-debt on Calvary, we tithe as an offering of gratitude. People don't argue over leaving a waiter a 15 percent tip at a restaurant; why then would we resent giving God a 10 percent tithe? What does it say about our priorities if we honor Visa before God?

Lie #4: All the church wants is your money.

No, we don't. We want fruit added to your heavenly account. We want to expose anything in your heart that will prevent God's blessings from overtaking you—things such as selfishness, fear, or greed. God's financial plan requires obedience, gratitude, and generosity. Generosity has nothing to do with finances. Generosity requires heart. It can be seen in a homeless man sharing his blanket or a grieving widow giving someone else a hug. You can give without loving, but you can't love without giving. On a practical note, churches have financial commitments too. Most people are comfortable with paying club dues or for seats to watch their favorite sports team. Yet they criticize a church that offers free services, free education classes, free parking, free child care, free music, and free coffee and doughnuts, but then receives a (freewill) offering?

Petticoats and Ferraris

It is normal for a father (and grandfather) to lavish genuine gifts on his children. My paternal grandfather rewarded each of his young granddaughters with a dress when we broke our thumb-sucking habit. My two older sisters both selected a conservatively priced dress. Not me! I spied a cheerful polka-dotted dress with a full petticoat and a matching Kelly-green coat. Yes, it was the most expensive dress in the department. Granddaddy never flinched. As a five-year-old I wore his love proudly. While my sisters teased me, they could have done the same thing if they had wanted.

On the other hand, most "Ferrari prayers" ("Lord, please bless me with a sports car") are fueled by selfish immaturity. I have often heard believers pray the most shallow, carnal prayers and then tack a Scripture verse on the end to justify their requests. A frequent example of this is the powerful promise found in Philippians 4:19, which says, "My God shall supply all your need according to His riches in glory by Christ Jesus." Slow down, Mr. Ferrari; this is not a carte blanche promise for your tainted treasures and misguided pleasures. Read in context, this passage finds the apostle Paul commending the Philippians' choice to put a priority on promoting the gospel. He is saying, "Because you guys gave your best offering to me not once but twice, I know that God will bless you big-time." That congregation in Philippi had a strong missions department that financed Paul's ministry when other churches had bailed on him.

Your Father loves you, but don't forget that you're on assignment. Tommy and I drive nice cars and live in a beautiful country home, but when He speaks to us about world missions, we are super-quick to obey. If I wanted a Ferrari I could buy one, but I would rather spend money on the gospel. I believe that when we get to heaven, we will all regret not giving more when we were here on earth!

A TOUR OF HEAVEN

After a woman died, St. Peter met her at the gates of heaven. "Welcome to heaven," Peter said. "This angel will give you a quick tour and take you to your eternal abode." The woman was eager to see it; one time in church she had heard about the mansions of heaven. Now, she didn't attend often, and when she did, she complained about the loud music and the long-winded minister. As they toured a row of the huge mansions, the angel didn't stop. As their journey continued, the woman noticed the houses growing progressively smaller until they reached a row of cabins and then a row of shacks. Finally the angel said, "Here you are, my dear; this is your eternal abode."

"There must be a mistake," the grumpy woman exclaimed. "Those are only two sticks leaning together."

"Sorry, ma'am," the angel replied. "That's all you sent us to work with."

The point of this story: don't underestimate the power of a seed. A seed is anything given to honor God. It might be a financial offering, a cake, community service, or intercessory prayer. If it's precious to you, then it's precious to God. Jesus made reference to this as He watched a widow give sacrificially. Once you realize that every seed brings a harvest, miracle moments become commonplace, some on this side of the grave and others on the other side.

Tommy appreciated this lesson years after having the distinct honor of hosting Lester Sumrall, the legendary apostle who traveled the world with Howard Carter and founded the LeSEA TV network, which broadcasts nationwide and internationally. Though gruff in his demeanor due to the eternal urgencies in his soul, Lester had a big heart. During their two days together Lester barely spoke a word unless he had a request for a specific food or question about the service. Tommy was surprised when Lester broke his silence one day to say, "I sure do like your shirt. Will you please go buy an identical one for me?" (This was in the 1980s when men often wore short-sleeved, open-collared "missionary/Hawaiian shirts" with a straight hem.)

Tommy felt a tad embarrassed to tell him we had bought that shirt at a discount clothing store for twenty-four dollars. Nevertheless, when we went to buy the shirt, they were sold out. We traveled all over Houston, frantically looking for something similar until we finally ran out of time. Too nervous to return without a shirt, Tommy asked me to wash and iron his, and he gave it to this respected man of God.

"I couldn't find one just like mine," Tommy explained when they met again. "So I took this shirt right off my back. Enjoy!"

Consumed with his Bible and books, Sumrall hardly acknowledged the gift.

"I refuse to be disappointed," Tommy said when he returned home. However, he admitted, "I thought that he'd be impressed that I gave him my very own shirt. He didn't even say thank you. But he represents world evangelism, so I planted it as a seed for a harvest ahead."

Twenty-five years later we received a phone call from LeSEA Broadcasting Network, inviting our son Andrew to air our new *Young Believer's Broadcast* on their network. As we rejoiced with Andrew, Tommy's smile grew somber. Tears suddenly rolled down his face, because the split moment he heard this good news, Jesus whispered, "The shirt." Jesus was telling Tommy "thank you" twenty-five years later. Friends, every seed is precious. God sees every seed, and every one brings a harvest. In this case, a twenty-four dollar shirt reaped thousands of souls.

Be encouraged today that although thousands of years have passed since Israel crossed the desert, God hasn't lost His recipe for manna. For forty years the Israelites received miracle bread, miracle meat, miracle guidance, and miracle protection, and then they received a miracle covenant that led them to a miracle land. That was in the Old Testament, recorded for our learning, as an example of the goodness of God.

Believers in the New Testament have a better covenant established on better promises. This brings me to a most logical conclusion: it is quite natural to expect the supernatural, and many of your miracle moments will include supernatural abundance.

Peter hosts Young Believer's Broadcast in 196 nations.

THE MIRACLE OF ABUNDANCE

God's work done in God's way will never lack God's supply.
—Hudson Taylor[2]

When you give because you cannot help it, you will receive because you cannot stop it.
—Wayne Myers[3]

God can trust you with material things when material things become immaterial.
—Tommy Burchfield[4]

Everything in your hand is a seed. Everything in God's hand is a harvest.
—Wayne Myers[5]

Beloved, I wish above all things that you would prosper and be in health, even as your soul prospers.
—3 John 2

CHAPTER 7

No High Like
the Most High

ஃ **Life Question:** How do I get free and stay free?

ஃ **Miracle Moment:** The miracle of the anointing

ஃ **Life Lesson:** Nothing takes the place of the anointing.

IF YOU ARE IN THE MARKET FOR UNSOLICITED ADVICE, TRY RUN-
ning a youth camp. Self-appointed experts come flooding out of the
woodwork, making such statements as, "Young people are different
today. You need to shake things up. You know, grab their attention.
After all, you're competing now with Hollywood and MTV." If their
opening salvos don't make us swoon, they follow up with other suggestions: "Why don't you add fog machines? Use ventriloquism with
your puppets? Tommy, if I were you, I'd really consider changing...
adding...building...blah, blah, blah."

Over the years it has been downright amazing to see how
many observers feel free to offer us advice on how to run Discovery
Camp. Of course most of these dear folks have never managed such
a facility. They don't have the first clue about how to keep grilled
food hot or dormitories cool for a thousand guests every week of
our sauna-like Texas summers. Their image of youth ministry likely
stems from visions of some Harvard-inclined overachievers singing
"Kum Ba Yah" around the campfire. News flash, folks! We're not in
Kansas anymore. Without exception, today's youth culture is tired

of the compromise and hypocrisy they have seen up-close in their parents' generation.

Certainly Tommy and I wanted to be teachable. Yet had we followed the advice so many offered, we could have slowly succumbed to changes that would have proven eternally tragic. After all, we constantly dealt with subtle pressure—both internal and external—to produce. Each summer we sensed the pressure to "top" what we did the previous summer. Each year had to be bigger and better than the last. This carnal pressure came to a climax in the year 2000, right in the midst of creating a musical production that would require a one-hundred-member cast. Just thinking about the energy required to pull off such a masterpiece exhausted me. Still, determined to step it up a notch, I plunged ahead. Thank God that my costumes, lyrics, and narration plans got interrupted by a voice that thundered inside of me. In that defining moment, standing by our gold couch, I knew that God had revealed the truth. It momentarily took my breath away and changed the course of our ministry forever: *nothing takes the place of the anointing.*

Nothing. Not musicals. Not lifeguards with perfect tans. Not flashy preaching. Not fog machines. Not hip-hop teams with the best rhythm. I then recognized the subtle deception involved when we depend on anything to reach people for Christ besides the sweet anointing of the Holy Spirit. To depend on fog machines or contemporary dancers to change lives is like the apostle Paul depending on his circumcision or good works to please God. That is a work of the flesh. I believe that truth demands a response.

That day Tommy and I renewed our commitment to act under the direction and control of the Holy Spirit. Our amazing staff supported us, although it proved difficult. We canceled some fabulous "shows" and cutesy singing groups, which didn't win us any popularity contests. We constantly faced pressure to promote Pastor So-and-So's niece. Still, we had to reach the place where we decided to only allow young people on the Ambassadors' Hall stage who were nurturing a heart for God. Our stage became an altar. Because of that, a fresh anointing invaded our services. Signs and wonders prevailed. Hundreds of souls responded at every gathering. Eventually we escaped the political pressure to promote VIP kids and instead directed them to the altar of the Lord. Just like five hundred thousand other campers who have lingered in His presence, they learned for themselves that there is no high like the Most High.

THE SECRET

So what is our secret to reaching people for Jesus Christ? How do we penetrate the gospel-hardened hearts of youth attending our events? How do we compete with MTV and the professional enticements of Hollywood? Tommy and I have spent three decades learning how to recognize and flow in the anointing of the Holy Spirit. It has been our secret to effectiveness. It can become yours too. We depend on the anointing in every area. We depend on this to draw them to camp and then to the altar. Yes, we still have skits, hip-hop, and even fog sometimes, but primarily as evangelistic bait. We don't depend on these fun tools. There is a huge difference between the Holy Spirit initiating a dance production and us attempting to create one on a deadline. When God does it, it's sooooooooo easy.

Let's face it: we can't compete with the glitz and glamour of Hollywood or MTV. The good news is that I don't believe God ever intended for us to do that. This is an apples-and-oranges situation. The glitzy performances entice the outer man, while the anointing touches the inner man. Glitzy entertainment arouses the flesh, while the anointing satisfies the spirit. I pity rock stars. Once someone sees Jesus in all His goodness and majesty, the best concerts will pale by comparison. So here is my message to parents, pastors, and others in any strata of society: *the Holy Spirit knows everything, and the Holy Spirit is always right.*

Read that statement again. Memorize it. Say it out loud, and you're on your way to success. Who is the Holy Spirit? How does He operate on the earth today? He is the Father's gift to us. God's gift to sinners is the Lord Jesus, our Savior. The Father's gift to believers is the Holy Spirit.

THE ANOINTING PROPHESIED

God has always had a plan—a progressive plan. As six thousand years of human history have unfolded, so has the role of the Holy Spirit. He is mentioned in both the first and last chapters of your Bible. That is significant. In the first chapter of Genesis He brings about divine order. In Revelation 22 He extends a heartwarming invitation to His bride, the church. Divine order and releasing invitations—those are who He is and what He does.

Old Testament saints knew of, and reverenced, the Holy Spirit. The miracles of Moses, the victories of King David, and the prophecies of Isaiah defined the nation of Israel. However, these people also understood that this divine power was reserved exclusively for God's "VIPs," namely the prophets, priests, and kings. Ordinary people were observers only, watching these miracles from afar through the big shots of their generation. Never would they dare expect a personal experience with the Spirit.

God provided several prophets a sneak preview of the end-times global phenomenon where He would pour out the Holy Spirit's anointing on all spiritually thirsty seekers. Isaiah said this anointing would destroy the yoke; Jeremiah compared it to a fire in our bones. Ezekiel prophesied that the wind of God would raise up an exceedingly great army. And though each of the prophets had a glimpse of the anointing falling on the world, Joel saw it in the greatest detail. Looking ahead 2,700 years through a prophetic telescope, Joel saw the unthinkable. Why, his priests would have forbidden it. What did he see? I like to think of it as a Discovery Camp Miracle Rally, with ordinary children and young people preaching, prophesying, and filled with the fire of God.

Here's what Joel wrote: "And it shall come to pass afterward that I will pour out My Spirit on all flesh; your sons and your daughters [at Discovery Camp and Texas Bible Institute] shall prophesy, your old men shall dream dreams, your young men shall see visions. And also on My menservants and on My maidservants I will pour out My Spirit in those days" (Joel 2:28–29).

Fast-forward seven hundred years from the days of Joel to AD 33, and you find one hundred twenty disciples of Jesus huddled together and waiting in an upstairs Jerusalem room. They weren't certain what they were waiting for, but He had instructed them to wait. Forgive my lack of theological correctness, but I like to imagine this epic event as follows: As Jesus completed His earthly assignment and sat down at the Father's right hand, I believe that He high-fived the Holy Spirit and said with a grin, "It's Your turn, My Friend. You have a tall order to fill. I told them that You were coming to be their helper, and I've promised them if they would do what I did, they will see what I saw. That includes loving who they call the nobodies and the Lazarus show." With a nod the Holy Spirit smiled, remembering the day He did the same thing for Jesus.

Suddenly on earth it happened! The sound of a mighty rushing wind and what seemed to look like fire fell on each head. What happened? The Holy Spirit moved from heaven to earth. As men and women were born from above, the Spirit gave birth to the church. Joel's seven-hundred-year prophecy unfolded, and the Holy Spirit, once reserved for prophets, priests, and kings, poured out on all flesh. *All* flesh. Males and females. VIPs and ordinary folks. God's favorite people, the Jews, and (*God forbid*) Gentiles too. To the Pharisees and religious rulers it was unthinkable and inconceivable. Yet, because it was God, it was holy, divine, and radically delightful.

Nothing takes the place of the anointing.

THE BIRTHDAY SONG

Can you see Jesus smiling as His promise to send the Holy Spirit to His disciples was fulfilled? Can you hear Gabriel's grand opera? They're singing the third verse now of an ongoing canticle. They sang the first to an audience of shepherds: "Christ is born this day in the city of David." (See Luke 2:11.) The second sounded on the Day of Pentecost: "Christ is born again in the hearts of men and women." (See Acts 2.) The third verse is still being sung to His church today: "The anointing of Christ is in you. Hallelujah. Hallelujah." (See 1 John 2:17.) The anointing moved to earth and gave birth to the church. What a birthday party! Instead of birthday candles, though, Jesus lit men and women on fire. The anointing no longer would come and go back and forth to heaven, but it would abide in the heart of this new species called "believers."

A "Who," Not a "What"

This anointing that gave rise to the church came from a Person with feelings, mood, and personality. The Holy Spirit's presence is what I refer to as *the anointing*. Understand that the Holy Spirit is a "who," not a "what." Scripture portrays Him as eleven types of emblems, which I will list here for personal study time later. The Bible describes the Holy Spirit as:

+ A dove: gentle and trainable (Matt. 3:1; 11:28–29)

+ A seal of promise: authoritative assurance of eternal truths (2 Cor. 1:21–22)

+ Equipping for ministry: dependence on Him required (Exod. 29; 2 Cor. 3:5–6)

+ Oil: provides illumination (Matt. 25:1–13)

+ Fire: provides warmth and light; purifies (Exod. 13:21)

+ Rain: watering seed, outpouring (Hosea 6:3; James 5:7)

+ Breath: providing eternal energy and motivations (Gen. 2:7; John 3:8)

+ Wind: the empowering life (Ezek. 37:9; Acts 2:2)

+ River of God: refreshing (John 7:38–39; Ps. 1:3)

+ Dew: growth (Num. 11:9; Ps. 133:1, 3)

+ Water: quenching thirst (Exod. 17:6, Ps. 87:7)[1]

John's Gospel gives seven titles for the Holy Spirit, each one adding a different glimpse of His magnificent being. Think of each as a job description: Comforter, Counselor, Helper, Intercessor, Advocate, Strengthener, and Stand-By. He is our indwelling Helper. If *you* don't need comforting, then He will help you comfort others.

If *you* don't need counseling, He will help you counsel others. He won't do everything for you, but He will help you. Remember, He's not the Doer; He's the Helper.

An example of this comes from a story about the mother who sent her ten-year-old son to clean his bedroom. Paralyzed by the mountains of clutter staring him in the face, the boy just sat and stared at the wall. His mother longed to do it for him, but she realized he needed to learn a vital lesson about taking responsibility. Still, she thought, "The moment he picks up about half of the clutter, I'll step in and help him finish." After poking her head into the room and spying a single dirty sock in his hand, she was filled with compassion. "Good enough," she thought, and charged in with a dust cloth and trash bags in hand. Together they accomplished the task in half the time. The boy was the doer, but Mom was the helper. This is exactly what the Holy Spirit does for us.

THE CHARACTER OF THE ANOINTING

The anointing is the presence of the Holy Spirit in a person, place, or thing. It is that supernatural, energizing force within a believer that makes the Spirit-filled life joyful and a person productive in Christian service. It was the secret to Jesus's miracles and the fuel for His earthly assignment. It represents a tangible, divine force, such as that seen in Acts 19:12, where Paul transferred the anointing into handkerchiefs and sent them out to heal sicknesses and cast out evil spirits. Now, sometimes you feel this kind of power, but more often you don't. Don't wait until you *feel something* to minister to someone. That is as foolish as saying, "I'm not going to eat until I can feel my gallbladder." Honey, you were born with a working gallbladder, so get busy eating your lunch. Likewise, when you were born again, you received the anointing to do the works of Christ.

When people make reference to "the anointing flowing through them," they are referring to the invisible, mighty person of the Holy

Spirit. I am reminded of a children's leader who brought a group of children to camp and had a vision of the Lord Jesus standing behind me. She said that He was reaching over my right shoulder to touch the campers I was praying for and they were all being healed. His hand was directly on my hand so that our hands looked as if they were glued together. She noticed that He was wearing white gloves. In a blink He vanished, but the white gloves were still on my hands. The anointing does the works of Jesus through us. Our hands are the hands of Jesus.

I love to watch people respond to the anointing. Some stand still like a wooden statue, while others shriek, wail, or run around the room. The experience is spiritual, but the response is in the emotional realm, so they will often cry, laugh, jump, or shake. I have had scoffers ask me if Jesus ever jumped or shouted. I'm not sure, but most of the people He touched did. I have watched hundreds of thousands of rebellious, gospel-hardened youth campers roll their eyes during the best Christian concerts, only to crumble like a house of cards under the presence of the Spirit. Sometimes the anointing is gentle as a dove. Other times He blows through a rally exposing sin, causing hundreds to fall under the power of God.

However, the anointing is not like a circus that performs miracles for spectators' thrills. I have seen many questionable theatrics in the name of the anointing, such as people instructed to stand in circles of ten and "vomit their demons" into brown paper bags. I have seen deacons running around a church to sweep gold dust that "fell from heaven" so they could pay off the church mortgage. (They later tossed this supposed gold because it got mixed with ordinary dust.) People, please! The anointing is not spooky, nor does the Holy Spirit put a vibrato in your voice. He is just as comfortable among choir robes as jeans and flip-flops. Like any other person, He goes where He is welcomed. In stark contrast, though, He brings miracles with Him.

The Anointing Is on the Word

To bring balance to the unconventional moves of the Holy Spirit at Discovery Camp, we have been careful to emphasize the written Word of God. It doesn't matter how high you jump in the Spirit if you can't walk straight when your feet hit the floor. As the West Texas expression goes, "The proof of the puddin' is in the eatin'," and after your *she-ka-la* times at the altar, you still need to submit to the Living Word. This is why I like to periodically pose a mischievous question to our guests: "How many would like to see a move of God—a miraculous, life-changing move of God—right now?" Most hoot and holler until I say, "Quiet, please. Watch me closely." Moving to another part of the stage, I slowly open my Bible and say, "Ta-da! Did you see it? Every time you open your Bible, God moves. Never forget that."

DC is four days of low-cost, high-energy, positive peer pressure.

Most guests feel ashamed that they are disappointed, but it helps instill a new reverence for the Bible in everyone. Such reverence is the reason for the common use of this phrase: "Please stand in honor of God's Word." Even if the Holy Spirit leads in a different direction and we have prophetic altar ministry, the team knows to share at least one scripture or a five-minute teaching. Why? Because the anointing is on the Word. When the corporate anointing lifts or people are home alone in a lonely bedroom, it is the anointing on the Word that will anchor them.

In 2002 I gained a new understanding of this as I quietly waited on the Lord to show me the right direction for the service. (Even though we have a planned program, the life of the Spirit must be paramount.) Suddenly the Helper whispered, "This morning will be a Luke 5:17 service." I was not sure what that meant, but as I turned the coffee-stained pages of my favorite Bible, He continued, "Begin by sharing My love and cast vision as you normally would. Then teach your prepared message, but be aware that I will be interrupting you." I was stunned when I reached Luke 5:17, which confirmed, "As He was teaching…the power of the Lord was present." Somehow I understood that the campers would not need to wait for the concluding altar ministry to be mightily touched.

I explained to the audience that it would be a Luke 5:17 service, so *while* I was ministering many of them would sense healing, deliverance, or the commissioning power of Jesus upon them. I instructed them to simply raise a hand as they would a baseball glove and receive their miracle. As I taught, I sensed an unusual anointing of the Word, and I noticed many hands reach up to "catch" their miracles. At the conclusion of the one-hour service, without any spooky music and with me in khaki shorts and sneakers, more than three hundred stood to testify of receiving authentic miracles. A sixteen-year-old girl shared how, when I said, "As for God, His way is perfect" (Ps. 18:30), she believed the Word. She wholeheartedly surrendered her heart to God, purposed to break up with her boyfriend (a distraction in her life), and accepted the call to world missions.

All of that occurred as a result of the anointed Word. You can see why the Bible says, "For the word of God is living and powerful, and sharper than any two-edged sword" (Heb. 4:12). Whether you feel anything or not, the anointing is always on the Word. My habit to prepare for teaching the Word is to study, study, and study as I get God's Word into my head. As I meditate on it throughout the week, it drops into my spirit. Then, as I wait on Him and pray in the Spirit, a specific topic or scripture bubbles up from my spirit to my intellect. This is how God gives me direction to lead each service. Sometimes it occurs during prayer, but at other times it happens while I'm drying my hair.

One July evening in 2004 my indwelling Helper reminded me of the story from John 21:11 about Peter's miraculous fishing expedition. After a fruitless night of fishing, when Peter and his friends threw their nets to the other side of their boat as the Lord Jesus instructed, they caught 153 fish. Right then the Lord challenged me to believe for 153 more souls.

"Tonight?" I asked in a wonder-struck tone of voice. "Last night was 'Salvation Night,' and we already saw hundreds accept Jesus."

Nevertheless, I obeyed, knowing that the anointing was on the Word. You guessed it: exactly 153 campers responded to the altar call. How cool is that? Such experiences are how I formed a personal strategy when I minister but don't sense any anointing—teach the Word. Read the Word. Sing the Word. Pray the Word. When the glory lifts, the Word remains.

THE ANOINTING: WHY AND WHEN

We can't confine the anointing to church buildings. Jesus healed three hurting people in the synagogues, but the other twenty-six healings recorded in the New Testament happened during His travels.[2] That should inspire us to share His love and release the anointing in workplaces, stores, locker rooms, and anywhere else we go. On several occasions the Holy Spirit prompted staff (at the oddest times) to walk into our woods or dormitories to make a security check. As a result, we prevented suicides, confiscated drugs, or brought healing to the brokenhearted. One afternoon our director on call noticed the go-carts were silent, so he made a radio call to check on the crew. The go-cart track manager replied, "Yes, sir, everything's fine. We're ministering the baptism of the Holy Spirit to a big group of junior high kids from Louisiana." The anointing even works on a go-cart track.

This is a holy gift, given for God's purposes. Exodus 29 confirms that the anointing comes upon you for the sole purpose of effective service, not so you can enjoy "Holy Ghost goose bumps" or achieve a prominent position. Jesus also confirmed that its purpose is to minister to hurting people. What colors are the hands of Jesus: white, brown, or black? You can find the answer at the end of your arms. You are the hands of Jesus, and if you will step out of your comfort zone, He will use you in a mighty way to heal, fill, and deliver people.

And my goodness, let's quit asking God to do something that He has already done. Instead of praying, "Lord, heal my friend of this cancer," acknowledge that Jesus became sick so she could be healed. Calvary is a finished work; Jesus accomplished everything needed for your healing. Don't talk to God about healing. Instead, talk to that spirit of infirmity (cancer) and command it to go. As you do your part in the natural, God will do His part in the supernatural. I would caution, though to instruct those who are sick to continue taking their medicine until a doctor has medically documented their healing.

Two Types of Anointing

The two predominant types of anointing found in Scripture are the corporate anointing and the believer's anointing. The corporate anointing is the Holy Spirit moving among a group; the believer's anointing abides inside a born-again individual. The corporate anointing comes and leaves for His specific purposes while the believer's anointing abides forever. If you doubt the validity of the anointing, just read the Bible:

+ Jesus said in Matthew: "For where two or three are gathered together in My name, *I am there* in the midst of them" (Matt. 18:20, emphasis added).

+ In 2 Chronicles 5:13–4 the presence of the Lord was so strong the priests could not stand.

+ In Acts 10:44 the Holy Spirit invaded Cornelius's house, and Gentiles were filled with the Holy Spirit.

These are Bible examples of the corporate anointing. My spiritual mentor Mama Ward had a cute expression after a powerful service: "It's amazing what God can do all by Himself." That's a good illustration of the corporate anointing. The Holy Spirit just moves in, does something eternal among the people, and then leaves.

Welcome the Corporate Anointing

Imagine sitting in your church and the queen of England walks through the front door unannounced. You would likely stop the service and honor her with a welcome and invitation to greet the people, wouldn't you? Shouldn't we treat King Jesus with the same kind of respect when His representative enters the room? Have you ever watched fog slowly move across a pasture? That is how you will sense the corporate anointing coming in to your midst: slow and gentle. It changes the atmosphere.

You will sense it more quickly if you are accustomed to private times of Spirit-led worship. When you sense the anointing, be quick to push your planned program aside as you give Him the respect and honor He deserves. He comes only where He is invited, welcomed, and worshipped. I usually stop and say out loud, "Holy Spirit, You are welcome here among us. We worship You, Father, Son, and Holy Spirit." Resist the pressure to "do something." Refuse to be rushed. Spirit-filled congregations with an unholy need to clap, shout, or dance just mess everything up. (Smile.) God can do more in one moment than you can do in a lifetime. Be still and know that He has come to reveal Jesus and help you do His works. If you're not quite certain what to do, lead the people in worship. After all, King Jesus is in the house, and His train (glory) fills the temple.

The Anointing Releases Miracles

Quite often, when the Discovery Camp altars got too packed for us to reach all of the campers, Tommy would simply wave his hand over them. Entire sections of teens would fall under the power of the Spirit. In July of 1992 almost three hundred children fell, simultaneously slain in the Spirit. In 2002 more than fifty children and leaders saw angels during a Miracle Rally. We interviewed each person privately; all shared the same exact descriptions and locations of our angelic guests.

That night I released this word of knowledge over eleven hundred youth: "You've just been initiated into a gang, and now you regret it. If you'll run to this altar, Jesus will set you free, and many will follow you." An awkward silence lasted for twenty seconds…then thirty. My indwelling Helper instructed me to resist the pressure to rush. Suddenly a commotion erupted in the back, cutting through the silence. Two hulking campers attempted to hold another boy down, but he finally broke loose and *ran* to the altar. During a heart-wrenching episode of repentance, the now ex-gang member sobbed, oblivious to the twenty-two other boys at the altar weeping. All later left their gang colors behind there on the altar as a symbolic statement of their decision.

One night a youth named Jeremiah Parks sat on the back row with his arms folded in apathy. After suffering years of horrific physical and emotional abuse by his father, he had a legitimate reason to be filled with anger and bitterness. Often his father put a knife to his throat or beat him severely. One evening his violent dad stuffed him into a black bag and hauled him to a field, telling him, "I've got someone coming to pick you up." Afterward Jeremiah learned this man he hated was not even his natural father. When this man died in a work-related accident, the boy thought, "Now I can live a better life." But he discovered the emotional scars had cut as deeply as the physical wounds.

Feeling like a fourteen-year-old nobody, he heard Tommy release the gospel of God's love. Jeremiah ran to the altar, crowded alongside hundreds of other youth. Pointing directly at him, Tommy said, "Young man, you are filled with anger and bitterness. You need to forgive your father, even though he is no longer in your life. And son, the Lord will become your Father and make you to become a man." A sobbing Jeremiah fell to his knees as a wounded boy but stood up an emotionally whole young man. Today he is a godly husband and father of three, leading a thriving ministry to orphans. Think of that! One word of knowledge and one miracle moment changed his entire life forever. That is the power of the anointing.

THE BELIEVER'S ANOINTING

In contrast to the come-and-go corporate anointing, the believer's anointing is the power of the Holy Spirit that abides in every born-again person, as explained in 1 John 2:27: "But the anointing which you have received from Him abides in you." What a thrill to watch campers learn that the anointing is already in them to do the works of Jesus. There is no junior Holy Ghost. Once youth "get it," it ruins them for the ordinary. Luke describes the believer's anointing most specifically in these words of Jesus (declare them over your day): "The Spirit of the LORD is upon Me, because He has anointed Me to preach the gospel to the poor; He has sent Me to heal the broken-hearted, to proclaim liberty to the captives and recovery of sight to the blind, to set at liberty those who are oppressed; to proclaim the acceptable year of the LORD" (Luke 4:18–19).

Being anointed is synonymous with being equipped for the task at hand. Anointing supersedes intelligence, gender, and position. The believer's anointing belongs to the believer. You don't need to beg for it because it resides in you permanently. I wish you could witness the miracles that happen when one thousand children or teens begin to "try out" the anointing. One night we invited two nine-year-olds to lay their anointed hands on one hundred forty children's pastors; most of the adults fell under the power of God. Young people crave supernatural power. They are disgusted with dead religion and dry Sunday school sermonettes. When they realize that God has saved them for the purpose of reaching and helping others, you'd better step aside and watch out. Usually God really moves, but sometimes wild fire breaks out.

"Wild fire" is an expression we use to describe funny things that happen as people learn about the powerful believer's anointing abiding within. Misdirected zeal is the worst nightmare for our structured, hyper-organized camp leaders. After teaching on activating the anointing, we challenge campers to go "practice." One service in June of 1999 comes to mind. God honored their faith and an explosion of faith consumed them. My! My! My! More than one thousand teens and adult leaders ran everywhere to bless one another. Those being prayed for would fall under the power of the Spirit. Campers jumped over limp bodies like they were playing hopscotch. Some cried hysterically while others laughed hysterically. I saw four NFL-size youth jumping and twirling like ballerinas, shouting and rejoicing in the Lord. Now you *know* that had to be the Lord.

How much of this activity did God prompt and how much was emotional? One disgruntled adult who said it was the latter apologized the next morning when he saw his group's most troubled teen delivered of crack cocaine and speak in tongues for an hour. Too much emotion? What do you think a rock concert is, or the Super Bowl, where fans shell out twenty-five hundred dollars or more for a ticket so they can jump around and scream? To those who think we're simply about emotional displays, I remind them that young people who came to us twenty-five years ago are now all over the world. They are bringing God's love and power to hurting people because of a "wild fire" experience that opened them up to the things of God. This real fire burned eternal changes into many of those young people. The rest left abuzz about what they saw. Here is my story, and I'm sticking to it: I would rather have "wild fire" than no fire. Such fire has also taught us how to build, bless, budget, and believe.

INCREASING THE ANOINTING

God wants to use you to demonstrate His love to others. Now that you know you received the anointing when you accepted Christ, recognize that you will learn to activate it by diligently studying God's Word and being fresh in prayer. Years ago I learned the importance of staying fresh in a humorous way. It happened after the words of the psalmist bubbled up in my intellect: "I have been anointed with fresh oil" (Ps. 92:10). All morning I rehearsed those final words: "Fresh oil…fresh oil…fresh oil." As my host drove me to the airport, she smiled, "Here's a tuna sandwich for the road." Tossing it into my suitcase, I forgot all about it. After an unexpected change of schedule, I didn't open my suitcase for three days. When I did, a foul stench took my breath away.

"That's what stale Christians smell like to me," God said.

Ugh. How nauseating.

Then I heard those words again: "Fresh oil."

I never want to smell stale to Jesus. Do you? Do whatever it takes to stay fresh in the Spirit. Decline unnecessary invitations or decline some time-consuming committees that waste more time on empty discussions than productive activity. Evaluate your music. Guard your affections. The enemy of God's best is something good. Slow down. Praise more. See others through God's eyes. Feel His compassion for people. When the thought hits you, "God could save that man," or, "God wants to heal her broken heart," recognize God's anointing. He wants to reach that person—and He wants to do it through you.

THE MIRACLE OF THE ANOINTING

The Holy Spirit is unpredictable, but never unreliable. There is nothing routine about the path of the Spirit-led intercessor.
—Arthur Wallis[3]

The Holy Spirit has come to reveal, to glorify, to magnify, to unveil, to exalt the Lord Jesus Christ....That's the occupation and preoccupation of the Spirit. It's what He does for a living.
—Leonard Sweet and Frank Viola[4]

I'd rather have wild fire than no fire.
—Rachel Burchfield[5]

The outpouring of the Spirit really is the Bible's cure-all.
—Bill Johnson[6]

CHAPTER 8

Bedpans and Bulldozers

᠊ᴥ **Life Question:** Do I really want God to use me?

᠊ᴥ **Miracle Moment:** The miracle of character

᠊ᴥ **Life Lesson:** What's happening *in* you trumps what's happening *to* you.

THE REVELATIONS ALWAYS SHOCK THE NATION. WHETHER IT WAS A famed political leader, movie star, professional athlete, military leader, or (sadly) pastor, in recent decades we have seen an endless series of private sins become public knowledge. Careers cut short. Families torn apart. Children wounded. Wedges of disillusionment driven deep into the public's heart. I name no names. I don't wish to point fingers, cast blame, or heap further insults on anyone. Still, these tales remind us that the race to greatness has many laps and high hurdles. Each one represents a contributing factor to the question of whether you will leap or limp over your earthly finish line.

The highly publicized falls from grace we have witnessed so often also serve as a reminder that there are four yous: the *you* your family knows, the *you* your friends know, the *you* you know, and the *you* God knows. The last one matters the most because He alone knows your specific race and the lane in which you will be most effective. Although many of our laps are similar, I can't run your race, and you can't run mine.

When you accepted Jesus as your Savior, God set a race before

you. Yours is your personal relationship with Jesus Christ. Period.
It is not your life's assignment or occupation. It is not your devotion to family or ministry. Ministers, it is not about the size of your
mailing list but the size of your heart. Businessmen, it's not about
your bottom line but crossing the finish line. It is the condition of
your heart when you have unplugged from the noise of the world
and you are all alone. It is the much-needed contrast between *what
you do* and *who you are*.

As you run your race, recognize that while people applaud charisma, God applauds character. Character isn't like a free gift in a
Cracker Jack box. It is developed by repetitive choices to honor God.
It pushes through the rubble of compromise with a determination
to do what is right, when it is right, and just because it's right. It is
as gold refined in the fire, building a greatness in you that neither
popularity nor adversity can tarnish. With that perspective in mind,
remember that every lap in your race is a continual response of what
I call Jesus's "Mark 12:30 Marathon Challenge," because this must
be the focus during our race: "You shall love the LORD your God
with all your heart, with all your soul, with all your mind, and with
all your strength."

OUR RACES

God prepared Tommy as a youth to run a race of character and greatness. He accepted Jesus as Savior at five years of age and—without
any instruction—was filled with the Holy Spirit in his mother's
back bedroom at age seven. His devoted Assemblies of God parents
instilled in him an appreciation for those in ministry. Quite often
they told him to look under his mother's bed so he could retrieve a
gift box containing a new suit for a visiting minister. His Sunday
morning routine marked him forever, as he stood at the kitchen
door for Me-Maw's careful scrutiny: clean hair, no dirt behind his
ears, belt buckle lining up with his tie, polished shoes, Bible, and an

offering in his hand! At seven he heard God say, "I've called you to do something great for Me." Know any seven-year-olds? They can hear God's voice!

Likewise the stained-glassed windows, four-verse hymns, and Gothic architecture of the Methodist church I attended growing up created within me a great reverence for God. However, at twelve years of age I learned that He was truly alive and wanted to live inside of me. There are millions of good, moral people attending church who are not born again. Previously I belonged to that group. But during my adolescent years the words of the hymns became God's *rhema* word to me. They were a musical Bible school that taught me about the joys of a Christian life. By seventeen I told God that I wanted to enter full-time ministry and begged Him to call me.

As an act of honor, to soothe my worried parents, I also became a registered nurse (RN), even though I could still say, as did the apostle Paul, "Woe is me if I preach not the gospel" (1 Cor. 9:16). When I was twenty-three, a minister informed me that God didn't call women, but he told me too late. I had already traveled across the nation, inviting hundreds to be saved and filled with the Holy Ghost. Tommy and I have both run our races strong, living whole-heartedly for Jesus Christ. By the grace of God we will leap over our finish lines.

Hurdles in Your Race

To an experienced runner hurdles are no concern. Yet when weariness or distractions occur, they can cause any runner to trip or get disqualified. I am listing eleven spiritual hurdles that you need to jump over in order to finish your race strong. Tommy and I have observed talented, anointed orators win thousands to Jesus and then trip over a hurdle of sexual sin or one of offense. While these hurdles don't cost you your salvation, they affect what I call the Eternal Awards Ceremony when the Lord Jesus distributes His "thank-yous" and "each one's work [your heart's motive] will become clear; for the Day will declare it" (1 Cor. 3:13).

HURDLE #1: The fear of man

The Book of Proverbs lists thirty-four benefits of walking in the fear of the Lord, while warning that the fear (applause and approval) of man is a trap. As Proverbs 29:25 puts it, "The fear of man brings a snare, but whoever trusts in the LORD shall be safe." Two personal experiences, one in junior high school and the other during my days as an RN, created in me a deep desire to know the fear of the Lord.

The first happened in ninth grade, when I was the tender age of thirteen. I had always been popular, but that year marked a defining season. I wrestled with whether to impress friends or please Jesus. After other students rolled their eyes at my newfound zeal for Christ, a popular girl started the "I Hate Rachel" club. Imagine the emotional trauma of sitting down for lunch and seeing everyone exchange knowing smirks before moving en masse to another table. The club steadily grew so dramatically that they flashed "I Hate Rachel" cards if I attempted to talk with a member. I ate alone for six days.

Finally, emotionally fragile and wounded to the core, I shook my fist at God and said, "You didn't tell me about this. My friends all hate me."

"Be quiet, little one, and listen," He replied.

I strained to hear. Something. Anything. Suddenly a distant sound reached my ears, slowly gaining volume and enthusiasm: a standing ovation!

"Lord, what is this?" I asked.

"Live for My applause only," He said. "All other recognition fades."

Peace and purpose flooded through my soul. Later God showed me that on that day the saints of old had been cheering me on. No matter. That day I purposed in my heart to keep my ears tilted toward heaven. Within a few days a teacher put an end to the club.

By the end of the year students voted me "Most Friendly." Many of the ex-Rachel-haters also accepted Jesus.

My bedpan ministry

During my brief nursing stint a supervisor required that I clean out some extra bedpans that didn't belong to my patients. While I knew this was unfair, I was just a young RN, and the older charge nurse was quite controlling. For several days I battled with the overwhelming stench, which made me quite grumpy. Finally I whined, "Lord, I know this is not the abundant life You've called me to. You've confirmed in my heart repetitively that I would be in full-time ministry and…"

Just then He interrupted: "Little one, will you clean that bedpan for Me?"

"For You, Lord? I replied. "Well, I thought You had more for me, but…I guess if this is what You want me to do, I will." As women often do, I added a P.S. to my prayer: "Lord, Your question really tilted me for a moment there, but I will be honored to clean bedpans for You. When I come through the Pearly Gates, You'll say, 'Welcome, thou good and faithful bedpan cleaner!'" Joy flooded my heart, knowing that I was doing something heartily unto the Lord. A few months later He released me into full-time ministry.

To do everything heartily as unto the Lord is to walk in the fear of the Lord. Whose applause are you living for? Do you have a life cause? Or do other people's opinions control you? On that final day we read about in 1 Corinthians, neither your spouse, parent, nor best friend will hold your hand. If you will always live to please God, you will find eternal reward and satisfaction. While others are chasing success, you will live a life of significance. As Proverbs promises, "The fear of the LORD leads to life, and he who has it will abide in satisfaction" (Prov. 19:23). He who walks before the eyes of God will never fear the lips of men.

Everyone has a "bedpan epiphany."

All people of character can point you to a critical moment when they gritted their teeth and purposed to serve someone "as unto the Lord." Tommy had a remarkably similar scenario working construction in his younger years. Digging ditches and driving bulldozers and eighteen-wheelers required him to rub shoulders with some rough characters. They cussed at him and mocked his love of God, but Tommy didn't shrink back. He learned to serve his boss wholeheartedly, regardless of the task. This type of "refiner's fire" burns up anything not authentic. As Psalm 105:18 says of Joseph, it will put iron in your soul. Don't despise these times! You are overcoming the opinions of others. Get to the place where you can boldly say, "I don't care who it separates me from or identifies me with, I'm going on with God." Remember, God is preparing you for greatness.

Hurdle #2: Self-control

Harnessing fleshly appetites is more important than a guardrail on a steep mountain road. God instilled your three primary appetites—food, sleep, and sexual intimacy—so don't let anyone frown on these pleasures. However, God also established preset boundaries for their use. They are not there to cramp your style but to protect you. Many people have benched themselves by neglecting these boundaries. Those who continue to step over them will traverse a road of slow destruction. Is the Holy Spirit speaking to you about harnessing your appetites? Whether you are sleeping too little or eating too much, take His promptings seriously. Whatever you feed will grow; sin thrills before it kills.

One time an internationally known evangelist wept bitterly in our office after an adulterous affair. He lost his marriage, ministry, and destiny because he tripped over this hurdle. While you can still find God's mercy, actions bring consequences. Sin will always take you farther than you planned to go, keep you longer than you planned to stay, and cost you more than you want to pay. Instead of giving in to urges, try making a "Psalm 101:3 Vow." What do I mean? When Tommy and I were dating, he had an unusual habit. Whenever we passed a lingerie store while out shopping, he quickly turned his head and looked the other way. I teased him until he shared with me his Psalm 101:3 vow to "set nothing wicked before my eyes." God prepared him even as a young man to guard his affections. Our marriage is strong because of it.

One of my self-control hurdles wasn't nearly as bad—or so I liked to rationalize. Yet as I listened closely, my Personal Trainer (the Holy Spirit) revealed to me the negative impact of excessive sugar. I can't tell you how many times I've heard other women's voices drip with emotion, affection, and pure desire when they uttered the word *chocolate*. I can easily recognize another sugarholic. Despite tripping repeatedly over this hurdle, I would say, "Well, it's not like it's adultery or cocaine. It's just a piece of chocolate cake. Right?"

Sin is whatever the Holy Spirit spotlights, and He told me I had a problem. Who knows? He may have been warning me against heart disease or another malady that wouldn't surface until my latter years. Honestly? I still trip over this hurdle periodically, yet hope against hope that broccoli will someday taste as good as my Ooey-Gooey Butter Cake.

HURDLE #3: Offense

During our first five years at Discovery Camp Tommy and I tripped over the offense hurdle several times. It usually involved church leaders who refused to keep their word or took advantage of personal friendship to escape from financial commitments. Lest I dig up the soapbox that I buried under the love of Jesus, let me summarize it this way. Because God called us to be "a friend to the local church," we have the lowest camp rates in the nation—typically 50 percent less than other church camps—plus we offer additional discounts for our partner churches.

Now, if a group gave us a final headcount of forty campers, we expected them to pay for forty campers. After all, we purchased food for forty people, reserved forty beds, and turned other churches away to prevent a dormitory from getting overloaded. Why is that so difficult to understand? Nevertheless, during our early years we often received mean-spirited letters saying we "needed to walk in love" and release someone from their financial commitment. Many times we did, but this trend toward sloppy business undermined our financial integrity and personal love walks.

For us it wasn't a monetary issue but one of principle. It *just wasn't right* that people made a commitment to bring forty campers and showed up with twelve. Nevertheless, we faced that offense hurdle multiple times and finally determined that we had to let God teach us to love. He told us to trust Him with the financial injustices. And that He could not only spank His own but also prompt His paymasters in the body of Christ to compensate. Today it is much easier to jump over that hurdle. Our partner churches try diligently to honor their financial agreements. When they experience a setback beyond their control, we work together in an honorable manner. Hey, you won't hear that *thud* from us tripping over a hurdle too often. Love never fails.

Love is not a feeling.

The Greek word for "offended" is *scandalon,* which is the same root word meaning "a trap." Your answer to offense should be to overcome evil with good. Walking in God's love doesn't come with goose bumps or fairy dust. It is not a suggestion but a commandment. It is the greatest attribute and the only one that never fails. Our great adventures of faith only work as we purpose to walk in love. So how is it humanly possible to overcome evil with good when you have been used, abused, ridiculed, or betrayed? You can't, but I will give you two tried and proven suggestions.

First, learn to say, "Lord, I've run out of human love. May I borrow some of Yours?" As you love by faith, His compassion will come.

My second suggestion is to genuinely ask another person about her childhood. I did this with a mean-spirited woman at our church. Because I asked, I developed a more compassionate understanding of her inner anger. It helped to know that her mother died when she was just six, a deep loss followed by her uncle raping her for seven years. In reality God brought that rude, deeply love-deficient, hurting soul into our women's ministry to receive a glimpse of His love in us. And she did.

Hurdle #4: Physical and mental health

The human body is a highly engineered masterpiece that confirms the superiority of our Creator. During my brief nursing career I saw firsthand the importance of caring for our physical bodies. Regardless of your spiritual anointing, you will find yourself hindered if your physical body can't keep up with life's daily demands. It needs exercise, rest, and proper nutrition. Burn the candle at both ends, and you will burn out twice as fast.

In the spirit of wise stewardship we must recognize that our bodies are a gift from God. We can represent Him better (and feel better) if we follow some basic natural laws, including taking responsibility for our health. Regular exercise, drinking more water, and thinking young make a prescription for long life. When I reached fifty years of age, I stage-dived for one thousand teens; at fifty-five I performed a cartwheel for a video project. With minimal life changes you can prevent or eliminate many diseases. Recently a special friend inspired me by attending an historic prayer gathering in Indonesia with one hundred thousand people. She maintained a grueling schedule of traveling, fasting, intercession, and teaching. Did I mention that she is still vibrant at the young age of eighty (same age as Moses when God called him to lead Israel to freedom)?

Mental health

Scientists are starting to catch up with the Word of God concerning the power of our thoughts. Research confirms that the brain is such a powerful masterpiece that, with intentional positive thoughts, new structures will begin to form and healing chemicals released. Winston Churchill was right when he said, "Attitude is a little thing that makes a big difference."[1] The average person has seventy thousand thoughts every day, and many of those thoughts trigger a corresponding emotion.[2] That is why thinking negative thoughts can throw your body into stress mode, compromise your immune system, and weaken your organs. Neurochemical chaos in our minds causes toxicity in our bodies. The bottom line is anything that gets into your mind will eventually get into your body.

This includes worry. Even though we know the detrimental effects of worry, Tommy and I have often tripped over that hurdle. (How well would you sleep if you had twenty thousand children and teens spending the summer with you?) Our phone rings periodically in the night, requesting prayer for campers who sneaked out, forgot to take their medicine, or fell off bunk beds onto a concrete floor. For years I would call our night manager before bed, asking him to *make sure* he had locked the swimming pool gate. We have seen Life Flight helicopters, sheriff's deputies, and many EMTs come and go, which can inspire fretting and concern. Yet we have also seen that God is faithful. We have sustained one serious injury among more than five hundred thousand campers. As the legendary spiritual leader Corrie ten Boom once said, "Worry does not empty tomorrow of its sorrow. It empties today of its strength."[3]

HURDLE #5: Fear

Have you ever had a headache and found yourself rushing to your computer to google "brain tumor"? Fear is a tall hurdle that can paralyze you from doing what God asks or becoming who God has called you to be. It will prevent you from the abundant life Jesus promised His children. The more it alters your life, the more you are in bondage. Realize that while psychiatrists have labeled five hundred thirty types of phobias, their root is the same. A spirit of fear will trip you up and eventually send you to the bench. In order to gain deliverance, get ruthless with your thoughts and refuse to give them negative ammunition. For example, when an ambulance passes by, you must refuse to text your teen driver just to check on him or her. Fear won't fade away on its own. It has to be cast out and replaced with faith.

We have trained hundreds of staff members to share their testimonies in front of campers. I encourage them to have one-minute and five-minute versions of what Jesus means to them. Yet many trip over the fear hurdle and refuse. One young staffer begged me not to make him speak in front of people. He promised to wash dishes for a month if I would release him from giving a one-minute testimony. Instead we taught him to resist a spirit of fear and insisted that he step out by faith. He was awesome and eventually shared God's love with thousands.

A gator in our pool

Located not far from the Colorado River, our home is surrounded by large oak trees. Hence, the name of our property: Great Oaks. One sunny May afternoon I was stunned to see a six-foot alligator in our swimming pool. An alligator! While waiting for the Department of Wildlife rangers, I watched this creature slither in and out of my pool. For the rest of the summer I didn't want to swim in it, reasoning, "Why, they swim so quickly that there's just no way I could get out to safety in time."

This fear controlled me until I severed it through the name of Jesus. I knew that if I couldn't swim with courage, then I needed to swim afraid. First, I put feet to my faith and swam scared a few times, constantly looking over my shoulder. Finally I realized God could release a rookie angel, one not even certified in Alligator

Patrol, to swat that intruder into the next county. Faith, which is agreeing with and acting upon God's Word, is your antidote for fear. And it will work every time.

HURDLE #6: Greed

Tommy often says there are three groups of people on the earth: the "Never Enough" bunch, the "Barely Enoughs," and the "More Than Enough" group.

Money trips the "Never Enough" and "Barely Enough" people up. They become a slave to money. They even work on Sunday in the name of responsibility but later suffer the consequences of pulling their family out of church. Some promotions are too expensive.

The "More Than Enough" crowd is those people who have purposed in their heart to live for God, and although they work responsibly, they do not work for money. They worship with their tithe and have linked up with the resources of heaven.

Tommy and I have lived in this group for thirty years. I have many stories about this. One involves a cute young camper who gave me a one-dollar bill for the offering she had missed while in the restroom. Sticking it in my pocket, I forgot about it for several days, until the Lord sternly reminded me of this holy offering. I quickly sent it to our financial department. Another time a woman gave me one thousand dollars as a personal gift, but as I opened the envelope, the Holy Spirit said, "This isn't for you or the camp. It's for a TBI scholarship." Two days later an international student called for assistance, and we gave him the good news. If you will become a channel with your money instead of a reservoir, God will funnel thousands of dollars through your hands. That is prosperity with a purpose.

One out of every six verses in the New Testament mentions a money-related topic. People are quick to claim that "money is the root of all evil," but that's not what 1 Timothy 6:10 says. It says the *love* of money is the root of all evil. There is nothing wrong with having money, as long as money doesn't have you. Tommy and I encourage realistic budgeting, savings accounts, and investments. Still, ultimately money is merely a tool to further the kingdom of God. Life is such an adventure when you know that you are blessed to be a blessing.

HURDLE #7: Character

Character is the *real you*, the one who surfaces when no one else is looking. People with character pay their bills on time, return borrowed items, and refuse to gossip or speak evil of others. They refuse to look at pornography or revel in Christian scandals. Their word is their bond, and they do what's right, when it's right, just because it's right. Genesis 39:1–10 tells the story of Joseph prospering and how his handsomeness attracted the attention of his master's gorgeous wife. She constantly tried to seduce him, but his answer demonstrated great character: "How then can I do this great wickedness and sin against my God?" (v. 9).

It is a sad indictment that evangelists have earned the reputation of telling gross exaggerations. Among ministers through the years it has become so common that we refer to this habit (tongue in cheek) as "evangelistically speaking." We came to the end of our third summer with a salvation count of 1,999. Yet each time I announced, "We had 2,000 people accept Jesus this year," I sensed the conviction of the Holy Spirit tugging at me. I didn't think it was *that* big of a deal to exaggerate by one soul. Apparently Jesus— who is the way, the *truth*, and the life— thought otherwise. So I asked Him to send me one more soul…any sinner off the street would do…but He didn't. For the next twelve months I carefully announced and rejoiced that 1,999 souls met Jesus.

During the first few years of Discovery Camp finances were one of our greatest needs as we built seven buildings. During that time, at one of Tommy's men's events, a gentleman recommitted his life to Christ after years of backsliding. That weekend he handed Tommy an envelope and said, "Tommy, this is a twenty-thousand-dollar check, which covers my back tithes. Use it to build this wonderful camp." Now, Tommy has strong personal convictions that the tithe belongs to the local church. However, an extra twenty thousand dollars would have sure been a blessing. And, after all, Tommy's ministry brought him back to Jesus, right? Wrong. Without wavering, Tommy replied (I heard him say it), "God bless you, sir, I appreciate your generosity. But that tithe belongs to your local church. Go home and bless your pastor." Then Tommy gulped.

HURDLE #8: Relationships

When the Lord wants to bless you, He brings relationships across your path. When the devil wants to destroy you, he also brings relationships across your path. We have watched godly young men surround themselves with corrupt businessmen who were driven by selfish ambition. These businessmen led those young believers right out of the will of God. I have seen wives so consumed with texting or Facebooking their BFFs (best friends forever) that they neglected their children and let their homes turn into pigsties. I suggest scrolling through your contact list and asking, "Does this person inspire me to pursue my dreams and live for Jesus?" Delete unhealthy and unfruitful relationships from your smartphone. Why? Because friends are like elevators. They either take you up or down.

HURDLE #9: Distractions

We once knew a brilliant man who set out to use his accounting degree to help churches. Tender to the things of God, for no fee he assisted ministries of any size. As a result he gained incredible respect. Eventually he started a business, but once it got rolling, he never helped another church. I believe that he got distracted from his original purpose.

A frequent distraction in churches originates with those who start their own ministry. You may have known people who sensed God's anointing while ministering at their home church. Enjoying the attention this brought them, they misinterpret this as a divine sign. Soon they are traveling widely, and speaking or singing at their home church only when they can take up a love offering. How sad. Those with the anointing must remember that God gives this for the purpose of building His church, not their ministry. It is possible that you tripped over the distraction hurdle.

While developing your talents will open many doors, don't allow yourself to get distracted. When you gain the world's applause or favor in the body of Christ, you can enjoy success. But in the light of eternity, don't stop there. Don't trip over this hurdle. Dedicate this talent to God and vow to fulfill His purposes. Make your stage an altar and give Him all of the glory. When "How Great Thou Art" morphs into "How Great I Am," it is time to head for the bench. The Spirit needs to talk with you.

HURDLE #10: Forgiveness

I have counseled women in great anguish after they suffered soul-crushing setbacks. I still remember the single mother who screamed, "I will never forgive him!" after her husband left her with four children to raise by herself. Those were the same words voiced one evening by a weary mother who had lost her beautiful daughter to a reckless drunk driver. Both endured heartache and grief too deep for words. Though broken through no fault of their own, they had to acknowledge this tough reality: Jesus said that if we don't forgive others, then our Father can't forgive us (Mark 11:26).

I explained to both mothers that releasing their anger and unforgiveness doesn't release their enemy from the "crime"; it simply puts the outcome into the hands of a just God. Eventually they forgave those who did them so wrong and today live joyful, purposeful lives. While anger is not a sin, failing to deal with it scripturally will give rise to a root of bitterness. When such a root reaches full maturity, the fruit will disqualify you from your race. Unforgiveness is an internal poison that will rob you of strength, joy, vision, and health.

I know because I have had to work through unforgiveness. It involved a family that had caused me deep, emotional trauma. I rehearsed in my mind the mean speech that I planned to blast them with. Fortunately I learned to turn this offense over to Jesus and forgave them. When we bumped into each other in the most unusual location, I embraced them and chatted as though we were dearest of friends. During my drive home I thought, "What did I do? I missed my 'mean speech' moment." Then I smiled, knowing that forgiveness healed everything, and I have asked Jesus to give them mercy.

Forgiveness is not a feeling. Often you must make yourself forgive, knowing that God's Word requires it. Think of forgiveness as presenting a gift to someone who doesn't deserve it. Meditate on the gift of salvation that Jesus gave you, one that you also didn't deserve. As you repetitively overcome evil with good, the Holy Spirit will supply the grace you need to truly forgive.

HURDLE #11: Trust

Unanswered questions, disappointments, broken hearts, and delayed promises will provide you the opportunity to face one of the biggest hurdles in your race. Many question how—if God is really a good God—something traumatic could happen to them. Be careful, dear one. God didn't promise a problem-free, peaceful stroll through life. Jesus told His disciples, "In the world you will have tribulation; but be of good cheer, I have overcome the world" (John 16:33). Once you begin to question the goodness of God, you will be benched for a great while.

As pastors, Tommy and I constantly help hurting people jump the trust hurdle. We see a continuing slew of setbacks and heartache. Let me give you a sampling of the prayer requests from our church family that crossed my desk one recent week: a son's suicide, a runaway teenager, a pregnant woman diagnosed with cervical cancer, a family's home that went into foreclosure, and a worried mother whose son is serving in Afghanistan. Why do bad things happen to good people? Because we live in a fallen world. There are no words to describe the depth of pain humanity feels, but you can't allow it to send you to the bench or even disqualify you from running your race.

Instead of meditating on the "why" questions, focus on the "what now." I understand sitting on the bench for a while to mourn your loss, but eventually life must go on. God wants you to trust Him with your disappointments and broken heart. He is faithful. You can trust His wisdom and kindness. As you say, "Father, I want to trust You," you will find yourself inching off the bench. When you say, "Father, I don't understand, but I trust You," you will reenter the race. Are you ready to leap that trust hurdle forever? Say out loud, "Father, I don't ever need an answer. I trust You. I'll serve You. I love You." Make the leap!

THE MERCY CLUB

Your response to each of these hurdles will bench you, disqualify you, or strengthen you for a great finish. At the end of the day the condition of your heart determines your race. A neglected grandmother who channels her self-pity into community service is an authentic Mark 12:30 marathoner. So is the Little League coach who makes kids think they are bound for the World Series. Remember, your race determines your eternal rewards, not your eternal salvation.

You might ask, "Rachel, what if I trip over a hurdle and fall down?" Here are two suggestions:

1. Join the Mercy Club with us.

2. Get up! Brush off those scraped knees and get back in the race.

Proverbs says, "For though a righteous man falls seven times, he rises again" (Prov. 24:16, NIV). When it comes to a runner who finishes the race successfully, it won't matter how many times he or she falls but how often this person gets back up.

THE MIRACLE OF CHARACTER

The measure of a man's real character is what he would do if he knew he would never be found out.

—Thomas Babington Macauley
English historian and statesman[4]

Watch your thoughts; they become words. Watch your words; they become actions. Watch your actions; they become habit. Watch your habits; they become character. Watch your character; it becomes your destiny.

—Lao Tzu
Chinese philosopher[5]

Fame is a vapor, popularity an accident, and riches take wing. Only one thing endures and that is character.

—Horace Greeley
American journalist and educator (1811-1871)[6]

Character is much easier kept than recovered.

—Thomas Paine
British-born American activist (1737-1809)[7]

Deep roots grow tall trees.

—Rachel Burchfield

CHAPTER 9

N-O-T-T-M-M

&> **Life Question:** How do I overcome trials and temptations?

&> **Miracle Moment:** The miracle of God's Word

&> **Life Lesson:** Put the Word in you when you *don't* need it, and it will be there for you when you *do* need it.

RECENTLY CARSON, AN ACTIVE FOUR-YEAR-OLD NEIGHBOR, WAS bitten by a copperhead snake—one of four venomous kinds populating the state of Texas. While snakebites are as common around here as a gully washer, victims and their families consider them anything but routine. Immediately the little boy's mother, Heather, a graduate of Texas Bible Institute, zipped me this text: "N-O-T-T-M-M!" This didn't represent a nonchalant response but a battle cry! Although their emotions were frazzled, she and her husband refused to move from their claims of healing for their son. They stood on the promises of God's Word. Although the doctor told them it would take seven weeks to recover, within six days Carson was walking. He amazed the entire hospital staff.

Heather cited a phrase she learned during her days at TBI, which originates with Paul: "But *none of these things move me*; nor do I count my life dear to myself, so that I may finish my race with joy, and the ministry which I received from the Lord Jesus, to testify to the gospel of the grace of God" (Acts 20:24, emphasis added). N-O-T-T-M-M, the acronym for "none of these things move me," is not just a ho-hum abbreviation. Paul included a list of afflictions he suffered, including shipwrecks, imprisonments, beatings, and eight different types of death-driven dangers, before he declared that none of these things moved him. A realization of the context of his words provides a much deeper appreciation for their significance. Throughout Discovery Camp's history, they have provided our family and our wonderful staff the determination to sink our proverbial teeth of faith into God's Word and—like a bulldog—refuse to let go.

Our Welcoming Committee

Our prolific opportunities to move away from the Word started the night we moved into the camp director's house on May 6, 1989. Driving down the driveway of what would become our home for the next fourteen years, we came upon the longest black snake I've ever seen. Stretched across the doormat of our home, this critter must have measured at least four feet in length. I don't like to get too spooky or off-the-wall, but in my mind there was no doubt who had sent it. It served as a reality check that, indeed, we were treading on unclaimed spiritual territory. Soon that snake slithered off, and I have never seen his type again.

If our slimy welcome weren't bad enough, we quickly discovered an infestation of scorpions in our new home. That first summer we stepped on at least five a day. One night I awoke with a start, alerted by the Holy Spirit to check Peter's crib. There I saw a huge scorpion, poised just a half inch from our sleeping six-month-old baby.

"Jesus!" I whispered.

The scorpion ran up and down, up and down, up and down, parallel with his tiny body, but it never touched him. In those frantic moments God brought to my memory the verse: "Behold, I give you the authority to trample on serpents and scorpions, and over all the power of the enemy, and nothing shall by any means hurt you" (Luke 10:19). While we trampled on both all summer, we left our shoes on. Those experiences taught me to make a fresh commitment to trust God with our children as I declared, "N-O-T-T-M-M!"

CAMP KITCHEN FIRE

"R-r--i-i--n-n--g-g!" Scrambling to find the phone in our darkened bedroom, I glanced at our digital clock, which blinked 1:04 a.m.

"Hello?" I mumbled, bracing myself for a prankster or a wrong number.

"Mrs. Rachel, the campers are safe," our administrator said, his voice giving evidence of a restrained panic. "And we called the fire department. But the kitchen is on fire."

Tommy and I rushed down the mile-long road to find more than four hundred children safely evacuated to the fields. Members of the Columbus Volunteer Fire Department were already at work. Though I remember flames flashing up thirty feet against the pitch-black sky, the rest of the night remains a blur. We awakened our staff and instructed them to assure the campers and leaders of their safety. It is always interesting how emergencies reveal character. While many expressed concern and kindness, one camper asked a staff member if their group would get a refund. And an exhausted leader moaned, "We just now got the children to sleep." (Remember what I said in the last chapter about not tripping over the offense hurdle?)

Satan aimed this fiery dart at us on Tommy's thirty-fourth birthday, which also happened to be the fifth birthday of our son Andrew. The devil's evil intent: temporarily shut down the camp. We believed it then and we still do. Long before the morning sun rose, we saw the obvious devastation. Not only had most of the kitchen vanished, what appliances and cooking area remained stood in three inches of soot and debris. People who don't believe in satanic attacks don't read their Bibles much or aren't much of a threat to the kingdom of darkness. First Peter 5:8 warns that "your adversary the devil walks about like a roaring lion, seeking whom he may devour." Fortunately Isaiah 54:17 assures: "No weapon formed against you shall prosper."

A few days later a representative from the Texas State Fire Marshal's office arrived, assuming we had shut down the camp for the duration of summer. It seemed obvious to a professional that reconstruction would require months. That wasn't what we thought. Shut down the camp? Disappoint three thousand more registered campers? Disappoint the parents who fasted and prayed for radical breakthroughs in their children? Turn away members from one hundred fifty partner churches? I don't think so! God's people don't shut down in times of adversity; they rise up! As Paul wrote, "Now thanks be to God who always leads us in triumph in Christ" (2 Cor. 2:14). I recognize there are times in life to stop and regroup, but we were certain this was an attack of the devil because we were so filled with resilient confidence and faith. We knew the truth that "He who is in you is greater than he who is in the world" (1 John 4:4).

PUTTING THE DEVIL ON THE RUN

Tommy and I sensed God's strength arising within as we prepared for the remaining three weeks of camp in that summer of 1991. Moms, realize that at this time our three youngsters were one, three, and five—not exactly the most convenient time to experience a fire! Thankfully the Lord sent a precious young woman to live with us, allowing me more flexibility. She wasn't the only blessing. Explaining our makeshift kitchen operations, we gave churches with reservations the option to cancel and receive a full refund. Not one of one hundred fifty churches accepted the offer, which sent a huge sigh of relief up from personnel in the finance department. Pastors and church leaders unanimously concurred that they didn't come for food but for the life-changing altar times. While God's people can sometimes disappoint any of us, when the chips were down they proved amazing. When we turned to the body of Christ, they rushed to our aid.

Still, as the reality of the challenge ahead settled over us, we found it tough to stay optimistic. In one of the challenging moments, when he wanted to run and hide, Tommy wailed, "Lord, what do we do?" The still, small voice of the Holy Spirit resounded: "Satan wants you to run in fear, but stand strong. Take courage and rebuild." Later Tommy wrote a mini-book based on the stand he made that day. He titled it *I'm Not Running From the Devil, the Devil's Running From Me.*

Our staff rolled up their sleeves and literally worked round the clock. Knowing that leadership involves presence, Tommy moved to the battered kitchen site and didn't come home for more than a week. Like Moses at the Battle of Amalek, he stayed where the workers could see him as they dragged out appliances for renovation. So could the women who—with mouth guards covering their faces and bandanas protecting their hair—swept out trash cans full of ashes and scraped soot with their bare hands. The suffocating smell of smoke permeated everything. We incurred expenses of more than one hundred thousand dollars, and the logistics of overseeing the restoration requiring Tommy's constant supervision.

Preparing three thousand meals each day with no kitchen was a miracle in itself. All staff housing turned into makeshift kitchens, filled with sandwiches and cinnamon rolls. Anyone with a working kitchen got used to the phone summons: "Please have four hundred corn dogs ready in one hour." Then vans rounded up green beans and corn dogs and shuttled them to the kids. Since our chapel doubled as the cafeteria, we had to set up and tear down tables twice a day to accommodate packed-out sessions of eight hundred fifty guests.

No matter what we faced, God proved His faithfulness.

Experienced electricians appeared, ready to help. Ministry partners and friends gave up vacation time to help relieve exhausted staff members. In the back of our minds Tommy and I kept hearing pessimistic reviews from the Texas Department of Health; one inspector warned, "It will take you six months to just get functioning again. Even then we may need to shut you down to get things into compliance." Imagine the fear this might instill if you were the camp director. Yet Tommy kept telling me privately, "We know this was a fiery dart from Satan. If we can't cast him out, we'll wear him out."

And we did. Our Miracle Rallies were more anointed than ever. The same spirit of faith that filled Nehemiah as he rebuilt the walls of Jerusalem consumed us. In just eight days we had an operating makeshift kitchen and defeated the devil! That summer camp finished strong because we refused to cower in fear and worked tirelessly. Was it worth it? These statistics are from the ten weeks of our third summer (remember, this was prior to any campus expansion). I will let you be the judge:

- Eleven thousand campers attended

- Four hundred churches from twenty-two states represented

- Two thousand nine hundred three salvations

- One thousand ten received the baptism of the Holy Spirit

- Six hundred fifty-nine accepted a call to full-time ministry

- One thousand one hundred thirty church workers and children's and youth pastors trained

Standing on God's Word continually provided the strength and guidance to finish strong. Though the enemy wielded a weapon against us, he did not prevail. N-O-T-T-M-M.

A Secret in the Battle

When attacks come, financial or otherwise, Tommy and I always sow something in faith and expect a harvest. Instead of running and hiding, we have learned to stand and give something as a seed of faith. The first thing we did that summer was to give away my car. Then we purchased three mobile homes for camp families. When the devil wanted to shut us down and run us off, we took the opposite approach and moved forward. Move forward! This is what God commanded Moses to do as he stood at the Red Sea with Egypt in hot pursuit: "Why do you cry to Me? Tell the children of Israel to go forward" (Exod. 14:15).

During our most discouraging moment a sleep-deprived Tommy stood on the chapel stage in front of eight hundred guests and instructed the staff, "Let it be known, I'm not running from the devil; the devil's running from me. Staff, go to the bookstore and bring every book and cassette tape in here. We're going to give away everything except the shelves." The service turned joyfully chaotic as pastors, youth pastors, and campers grabbed free books and tape series worth thousands of dollars. What a visual lesson on spiritual warfare! We were throwing entire tubs of mini-books into the crowds, and they were catching them like Frisbees. It was wild, wonderful, and vintage Tommy. Do you understand that we weren't just giving books away? We were sowing them into the very people we wanted to strengthen. When you sow a seed in faith, you always reap a harvest. You might say, "Rachel, I can't afford to do that." Well, when you're in a battle, you can't afford not to.

Not every setback is a satanic weapon. People sometimes break natural laws or make unwise decisions and then want to blame the consequences on the devil. As you grow in God, you will notice that with a true attack from the kingdom of darkness, a supernatural fight and resilient faith will rise up in your spirit. Don't run or yield to fear. Stand in faith. You too will put the devil on the run.

THE TINY CHIHUAHUA

Have you heard the story about the man who owned a little Chihuahua named Chico? Each evening they walked down the block happily until one day when they passed a large hacienda with a German shepherd. A single bark from that hulk sent Chico racing back to the safety of his owner. Day after day this occurred until one time, without explanation, Chico had finally had enough. Just before the German shepherd released his intimidating bark, Chico lunged toward him and let out a shrill, repetitive series of "yip-yip-yips." The big dog came to a screeching halt, tucked his tail between his legs, and ran back to his yard. Chico smirked and sauntered back to his stunned owner. The moral of this story: it's not the size of the dog in the fight, but the size of the fight in the dog.

Sometimes we felt like that little dog, facing German-shepherd-size opponents barking fiercely at our Chihuahua-like resources. One example involved juvenile court authorities from Maryland, who put a young man on probation on the condition we oversee his rehabilitation. Miraculously delivered from drug addiction, this young man became a strong preacher while working in construction. One day while roofing our four hundred-seat cafeteria, the Blue Jean Café, he slipped and fell headfirst toward the concrete eighteen feet below. Just before he hit the surface, his body oddly turned. On impact he only broke an ankle. He shared later about feeling unseen hands flip him like a pancake. A weapon came, but it didn't prosper. N-O-T-T-M-M!

During one camp session tornadoes hopscotched through our region. We herded thirteen hundred teens into a pitch-dark chapel with no lights, no sound system, and no air conditioning in oven-like conditions as we did our best to calm them through four hours of torrential thunderstorms. Without the peace and clear instructions from the Holy Spirit, I am certain that mass hysteria would have prevailed. The next morning we learned that tornadoes had touched down on both ends of the property but only damaged some trees. God's keeping power prevailed. A weapon came, but it didn't prosper. N-O-T-T-M-M!

BETRAYAL

If you will say this next sentence out loud and believe it in your heart, you will instantly grow in God: the Holy Ghost knows everything, and the Holy Ghost is always right. Say it twice more and purpose in your heart to obey His promptings. After all, He is your Helper, and He knows every detail of your day—and destiny. He certainly helped us once with what could have become an exasperating experience.

At 3:00 a.m. the Holy Spirit awakened Tommy. Hearing an odd noise outside, he saw the silhouette of a vehicle with its headlights off driving away from campus and pulling a loaded trailer. When the vehicle drove past a streetlight, Tommy recognized the driver: our food service director. She was sneaking off in the dark of night, leaving us no notice of her resignation. (Sad that some people make inconsiderate, irresponsible choices.) However, it is comforting to know that the Holy Spirit's promptings can prevent or often alleviate the effects of such actions. We awakened several staff members who normally reported to the kitchen at 4:30 a.m., and they responded enthusiastically, meaning our new TBI student body had a hot breakfast waiting for them that morning. We stayed one step ahead of the devil. He hurled a weapon of chaos at us, but it didn't prosper. N-O-T-T-M-M!

DEATH THREAT

One day Tommy and I received a letter filled with hateful threats. Any employers who have fielded correspondence from disgruntled consumers or angry former employees can relate. However, this letter was different. It contained a tone of evil. Alarmed, we called the police. Within twenty-four hours they had referred the matter to the Federal Bureau of Investigation. Saying that we were looking at a possible death threat, they instructed us to never be alone and scan the crowd whenever we entered Ambassador Hall, looking for anyone we recognized who might be bent on revenge.

While Tommy refused to cower, the threat controlled me for four months. Instead of arriving early at services to talk with guests, I would arrive at the last minute. While thousands were lost in worship, I kept my eyes open, watching and waiting for evil to explode. I repeatedly rehearsed in my mind management mistakes at Columbine High School. Or I mulled over our risk management codes—just in case. Although no one knew why, I constantly checked on our children's locations. Such is the nature of fear. It takes up residence in the shadows and then slithers into every area of your life. Fear persuades you to do things "just in case," like carrying detailed medical information in my wallet and regularly leaving services early.

I didn't broadcast my fears. Not even Tommy knew that this death threat hampered my functioning as a leader since I continued to smile and act strong for our young people. Finally I cried out to the Lord: "It's difficult to enjoy these camps when I don't know where 'he' is." Instantly He replied sweetly, "Peace. I know where he is, and he needs your prayers." That one comment changed everything; my fear melted into a puddle of compassion. Ten months later the FBI contacted us with the results of their investigation. The teen sender turned out to be a troubled camper from New Mexico who wanted to play a prank. I admit that a weapon of fear did chip at my shield of faith for a while, but in the end it didn't prosper. N-O-T-T-M-M!

You may not encounter this kind of cruel threat, but remember that Satan hates anyone doing God's work. He aims at those who decide to live by faith and rescue hurting people from his grip. While he may not target you personally, he still hates the Word abiding within you. He hates that you are God's masterpiece. Yet this hate should never deter you. Why? Because the devil is a defeated foe. Despite the attacks we faced, like Shadrach, Meshach, and Abednego we barely smelled the smoke from fires, tornadoes, lawsuits, false accusations, suicides, and even worse. While Satan's weapons have been too numerous to record, why would we ever want to?

Don't get caught up in reciting all the bad things that have happened to you. Long-term faith perseveres. We are living in a time when people worship convenience over conviction. Immediate gratification trumps long-term goals. This was not the case with past generations who blazed the trail for Christendom. They remind us that God is looking for soldiers, not sissies. The most prolific writer of the New Testament, Paul, issued our battle cry: "You therefore must endure hardship as a good soldier of Jesus Christ" (2 Tim. 2:3). Get strong in the Lord and prepare for opposition, recognizing the world martyrs more Christians today than during the first century. If you will allow me to offer a modern phrasing of Scripture, it would be, *"Thus saith the Lord, 'Toughen up, Buttercup!'"*

FOR WOMEN ONLY

We females in particular need to continually refuse to be influenced or controlled by anything (or anyone) except the Word of God. Many voices compete for final authority in our lives. It can be our moods and emotions or others' opinions. One woman recently told me, "I knew that I was gonna have a bad day as soon as I spilled tomato juice on my blouse." How revealing. Had she been anchored in the Word, she might have thought, "Praise God, now I can go buy a new blouse and the clerk will probably get saved."

People joke about women and our mood swings, like the husband who—when asked if he ever woke up crabby—replied, "No, I just let her sleep." However, we need to let the Word of God dwell in us until it stabilizes our moods. Once I chatted with a noticeably grumpy friend. When I asked, "What's wrong?" he replied, "I dunno. I guess it's just 'that' day of the month." Evidently he had a woman in his life who allowed her moods to control her. She needed to hear the good news that Jesus is Lord over every day of the month.

FOR MEN ONLY

Once a businessman told us of getting stressed out because the stock market was going down and his bathroom scales were going up. Men have a tendency to be controlled by doctor's reports, bank statements, demanding employers, or inconsiderate spouses. Just as women need to avoid moodiness, so do men. They need to realize that they can walk in perfect peace when the Word of God is their final authority. When men determine to live by the Word, they will no longer be controlled and shaken by circumstances or feelings. They will become like a cork that can't sink. The Word inside will cause them to rise in every situation.

EATING THE WORD

Emperor Menelik II was an African ruler who defeated the Italian army at Adwa in 1896 and became one of Ethiopia's most famous rulers. Since he believed the Bible had the power to cure illness, he ate a few pages any time he felt sick. After suffering a stroke in 1913, he ate the entire book of Kings. The pulp obstructed his bowels and he died of related complications.[1] The good emperor was right about one thing: The Bible is a miracle book. However, had he studied

2 Timothy 2:15, he would have learned that it is food for the soul, not the stomach.

A better method of getting healed is to practice Tommy's legendary statement: "Put the Word in you when you don't need it, so it will be there for you when you do need it." This one phrase has inspired thousands to a habit of lifelong Bible memorization. The Word of God, which is forever settled in heaven, will stabilize the most tumultuous situation. I suggest that you learn the precious promises *before* your well-meaning doctor, banker, or relative gives you a negative report.

Remember, the Word is more precious than the gold that prompts men to take ill-advised actions. On January 4, 1848, James Marshall picked up a piece of metal at the Sutter Mill in California that experts later confirmed was gold. Over the next decade "Gold Fever" inspired one hundred thousand people from around the world to travel to the West Coast with hopes of discovering instant wealth. Instead, many suffered great hardships, like the eyewitness who wrote a letter that included this statement: "Of our ill success you have probably been informed (and) consequently of our long stay there, (and) of the deaths in our party. Yes, here (three men) yielded up their breath to God who gave it."[2]

Similarly, how many in modern days have gambled away small fortunes in vain hopes of winning a Powerball jacket or beating the steep odds at a casino? Instead they should have searched for riches that won't fade away. In the Psalms David says God's Word and judgments have the highest value. He said they are so precious that "more to be desired are they than gold, yea, than much fine gold; sweeter also than honey and the honeycomb. Moreover by them your servant is warned, and in keeping them there is great reward" (Ps. 19:10–11). The diligent Bible reader will uncover such rewards as guidance, cleansing, spiritual food, healing, stability, wisdom, and peace.

Just as miners learn to depend on the light attached to their hat, skilled Bible students learn to depend upon the Holy Spirit for illu-mination. Most Bible truths don't lie on the surface. However, with patient, daily discipline, the Holy Spirit will enable you to dig until He reveals the truths designed specifically for you. A diligent student learns to mine the treasures in the Word. One flash of His truth can expose dead ends and guide you in a new direction. This is why you shouldn't rush through the Bible. Slow down and ask the Holy Spirit any questions you have about the verses you are studying. Follow any promptings to turn to another scripture, or another, then another. You are on a treasure hunt, and the Holy Spirit is your personal guide. As He reveals nuggets of gold, remember it's not what you *know*; it's what you *do* that helps you grow.

Kenneth Copeland dedicated our Ambassador's Hall in 2004.

A SWEET HABIT

Developing the habit of memorizing God's Word is most beneficial. I have known ten-year-olds who can quote entire chapters. It will take only a few minutes each day to learn one scripture per week. Consider it to be holy homework. I recommend the "M&M" method, where you *memorize* a scripture for four days and then *mediate* on it for the next three days. Here are some tips.

+ **Memorize:** Purchase some index cards and commit to study them just five minutes per day. Write out or type the verse(s) and scatter them around your home and office. I work on my memory verse while I'm walking on the treadmill or blow-drying my hair. You will not feel any goose bumps or sense the anointing until later when it becomes as a missile shooting out of your spirit to knock down a fiery dart.

+ **Visualize:** Focus on a word picture that might be in your scripture. Psalm 23 describes green pastures. How large are they? How tall is that grass?

+ **Emphasize:** Say a scripture out loud by emphasizing a different word. For example, Psalm 23:1 would go like this:
  "The LORD is my Shepherd…"
  "The Lord IS my Shepherd…"
  "The Lord is MY Shepherd…"
  "The Lord is my SHEPHERD…"
  Each phrase helps sheds a different perspective and meaning, which will come as you memorize and visualize each word.

+ **Personalize:** What a great discovery when you realize the Bible is God talking to you personally. Try putting your name (or a loved one's) into a scripture:
  "No weapon formed against [Michael] shall prosper" (Isa. 54:17).
  "He who has begun a good work in [Michael] will complete it" (Phil. 1:6).

Be patient as you learn the skill of memorizing and meditating on God's Word. Your mind will try to wander off to other thoughts—not necessarily bad thoughts, just nagging "Did-I-remember-to-plug-in-my-cell-phone?" type thoughts. This process will become easier as you train your brain.

Parents, think of this as your most important daily task. When our three children were growing up, I gave each of them a "Courage Card" each Monday morning. We read these scriptures out loud several times while driving the eleven miles to school. By Friday they were quite familiar with them. Try not to preach, share, or elaborate about God's Word. Just read it to your children, knowing that it will convert their souls (according to Psalm 19:7) and create within them a desire to know God. There will come a day when you must release them to make their own choices. Even if they endure a "Season of Stupid," you can still trust the Word that you have put into their minds.

CHEWING ON THE WORD

Cows can teach us a good lesson on memorizing and meditating on God's Word. We have a lot of cows in Texas; as I write this, I'm staring at fifteen Herefords in our pasture that belong to a friend. Cows have two stomachs, each with two chambers. Their morning grass goes into the first chamber, known as the rumen. The rumen is full of good bacteria, which helps soften and digest the food. From there it moves into the second chamber, the reticulum, which softens the food further and forms it into small lumps of cud. A few hours later they sit down and regurgitate the morning grass and chew on it some more. (For city slickers, this is known as "chewing your cud.") This process continues as the cow extracts flavor and nutrients and swallows it again. Then the third chamber, the omasum, processes the cud further and filters it so it can move into the abomasum.

This fourth chamber works similar to the human stomach, finally digesting the food with stomach juices.[3]

Just as a cow carefully and methodically digests its food, so we should memorize and meditate on our spiritual food. Memorization is like a cow eating grass. Meditating (thinking, pondering, and savoring) is like a cow that chews its cud. Both are yummy. (Pre-chewed grass may not sound too delicious to you, but the cows love it.)

A POWERFUL MISSILE

I liken the Word to missiles, whether guided, ballistic, or cruise missiles. As powerful as these weapons are, they don't compare with the power of the Word. It contains the greatest force of the universe. The second greatest force? The Word in your mouth. Christianity is often called "the Great Confession." While some teachers have gotten out of balance with this concept, confession simply means to agree with God. As Proverbs says, "Death and life are in the power of the tongue" (Prov. 18:21).

Imagine God looking over the balcony of heaven with a pair of binoculars as an angel asks, "What are you doing, great Jehovah God?"

"I'm looking for My Word, so I can release My miracle power upon the earth—healings, deliverances, and great revivals."

"S-o-o," responds the curious angel, "What do you see?"

Clearly disappointed, the Lord answers, "I'm seeing a lot of opinions, soapboxes, and sermonettes, but I can't fulfill those. It's only My Word that I watch over. I only perform My Word."

Whether a teenager or an aging tycoon, decreeing the Word works! God is watching for it and will perform it every time. Hell cannot annul what God declares in heaven. I saw an apt reminder of this during one of our "Talent Quests," a feature of every Discovery Camp session. A seven-year-old boy with two missing teeth auditioned, not realizing that he had to excel in something. Bless his heart, the lad couldn't sing, dance, or even spin a yo-yo. So I asked him, "Everyone is good at something. What's your talent?"

He decided that his best talent was quoting the Word of God. So off he went without any introduction, saying, "Deuteronomy chapter twenty-eight thez, becoth I have diligently lithened to the voith of the Lord, I am blethed going in, blethed going out, and the Fruit-of-my-Loom is blethed." He may have sounded funny, but his words were true!

Praying the Word is not just repeating scriptures like a trained parrot. Nor is it a formula. It is the Holy Spirit revealing the will of the Father to the heart of His child and releasing the faith to agree with Him for an answer. Paul provides some guidelines in Ephesians, where he writes about putting on the armor of God: "And take...the sword of the Spirit, which is the word of God; praying always with all prayer and supplication in the Spirit" (Eph. 6:17–18). Look at that verse closely and ask yourself, "Where is that sword of the Spirit?" In your hand? Does God's Word in your hand resist the devil? No, it is in your prayers. When you speak it in your prayers, the Word becomes a sword of the Spirit. As you learn to pray the Spirit-selected scriptures in offensive faith instead of defensive fear, that sword gets sharper and sharper. Paul says that our shield of faith will quench all the fiery darts of the devil. That means all.

Angels in the Doughnut Shop

There is an old joke about a doughnut shop filled with bored angels just sitting around. "I wish that I had something to do today," Angel #67435 whines, "but I've been assigned to a guy that doesn't even believe I exist. By the way, where's Angel #87987 been lately?"

"Didn't you hear?" replied another angel. "His client found Psalm 34:7 and started to get #87987 busy. Then he learned that Jesus was his High Priest, and things are so wild that our heavenly homeboy is asking God for reinforcements."

I hope this story brought a smile to your face, but it is probably truer than you realize. While Jesus is the High Priest of our confession, you need to give Him something to work with. If you are always confessing, "I'm sick and tired and nothing is going my way," I believe Jesus just shakes His head and says, "Holy Spirit, please get that Burchfield book over to them so they can learn My ways." However, if your morning prayers are full of the kind of faith that declares, "Lord, because of what You've done for me at Calvary, I am blessed; I'm not a beggar, I'm a believer...I am thanking You in advance for saving my entire household, according to Acts 16:31, and opening doors of favor with my boss, according to Psalm 5:12," that blesses me. Jesus, your High Priest, presents those confessions before the Father, and He fulfills His Word on your behalf and for His glory.

The bottom line: don't be moved by negative, fearful reports, bad symptoms, or evil threats. The correct acronym for FEAR is "false evidence appearing real." Honor God's Word. His character stands behind His Word and settles a matter forever in heaven. The first and last things Jesus said to the devil were, "It is written" (Matt. 4:4) and "It is finished" (Rev. 21:6, NLT). Tommy often says, "If you can find where 'It is written,' you can tell the devil 'It is finished.'" Be diligent to read, memorize, meditate, pray, and confess God's Word daily. No weapon formed against you will prosper. No matter what comes your way, you can declare boldly N-O-T-T-M-M!

THE MIRACLE OF THE WORD OF GOD

God's Word is sometimes a map, a love letter or a missile, depending on your need.

—Kenneth E. Hagin[4]

The Bible is a book about a Father and His family.

—E.W. Kenyon[5]

The New Testament is the most remarkably preserved book in the ancient world with almost 5,656 Greek manuscript portions in existence.

—Josh McDowell[6]

A Bible which is falling apart is usually owned by someone who is not.

—Frances "Mama" Ward[7]

The Bible is the Constitution of Christianity.

—Billy Graham[8]

The Old Testament in one word: do. The New Testament in one word: done.

—Rachel Burchfield

The Bible is the only book where the Author is present at every reading.

—Anonymous[9]

CHAPTER 10

Many Sons and Daughters

ঌ **Life Question:** What seven disciplines are needed for spiritual maturity?

ঌ **Miracle Moment:** The miracle of discipleship

ঌ **Life Lesson:** First, you make your habits, and then your habits make you.

AS OFTEN AS UNEXPECTED PHONE CALLS HAVE AWAKENED ME in the middle of the night, you would think I would be used to them, but I'm not. I seem to remember each one, including the specific time of the call. One jangled me from my sleep at 2:34 a.m. When I answered, I heard the Mississippi accent belonging to my beloved husband, who had enthralled me now for seven years, saying, "Sug, I'm in the London airport on a layover, and I need to tell you something." As his voice drifted in and out over our crackling overseas connection, I felt certain he was about to tell me how much he loved me, but that never crossed his mind. He continued, "I've heard from God. It's time to begin our Bible school, and you're supposed to be the president."

Click! The connection sputtered out. I waited for a return call, but he had to rush off to catch his next flight. Bible school? Now? Since we had discussed this previously, the news itself didn't shock me, but God's timing that April day of 1990 certainly did. After all, we had two sons under the age of four, and I was carrying our third child, a daughter. Knowing that to start something eternal I needed a prayer room more than a notebook, I pondered and prayed about his message. Before he returned, I was pregnant with two babies: Abigail Lee and Texas Bible Institute.

Tommy had called me returning from Lagos, Nigeria, where he had traveled as the guest of a special friend conducting a crusade. During the visit Tommy had the unforgettable experience of preaching to tens of thousands of young people and watching them respond enthusiastically to the Word. One stormy night they stood through hurricane-force winds to hear about this God of love and power. This sea of beautiful black faces begging for the Word of God is forever etched in Tommy's memory. Afterward these kids chased after the host's Volkswagen, crying, "Brother Tommy, Brother Tommy, take me to America!" During that moment God spoke: "Go home and begin the Bible school."

Sometimes God provides highly detailed commissions, such as when He instructed Moses in building the tabernacle. At other times He tells you to just start and the plan unfolds as you go. Establishing TBI brought a mixture of both, with Tommy always carrying around a yellow legal pad to jot down any divine inspirations or ideas. God directed us to tailor it for ages seventeen to twenty-five and teach Christian foundations, which gave rise to our *Foundations for Life* curriculum.

The unanswered questions outranked the clear details. After all, who was going to teach all these classes? Cook students' food? What about lodging? What is a fair tuition? What will keep them busy when they are not in class? And my big one: How am I going to do this with three young children in tow? Despite my misgivings, I sensed total assurance that God would guide me. If I would wait on Him, His plans would unfold and prove far superior to mine.

SMALL BEGINNINGS

Forty students enrolled in TBI's charter class—sort of. Twenty-five enrolled, and we volunteered our staff as students so we could practice on them, offering them free tuition so they could stay on after camp. To paraphrase Zechariah 4:10, this was definitely a "despise not the day of small beginnings" season. One day I passed a student walking down the camp road. I stopped to ask where he was going and he replied, "I'm quitting and walking home." When I asked where he lived, he said, "Louisiana!" I put him in my car and talked some sense into him. Because so many of our students worked in food service, half left in the middle of class to prepare lunch. The other half typed the tests, so not surprisingly the next day they would make an A-plus on them.

More than two decades later personal discipleship and Bible foundations still mark the cornerstone of our program. (Beginning September 2013 TBI will begin two new four-month programs to offer either basic discipleship or leadership training.) Young people today deal with such raging cultural issues as social drinking, convenient access and nonchalant attitudes toward abortion, and homosexuality. Serious, life-threatening issues, such as eating disorders and unchecked emotional outbursts, are candidates to affect their health, future marriages, and careers. Restoration and deliverance don't always come via a minister's anointed hands. It often takes time and renewing one's mind to overcome the pain of abandonment or the anger of being raped by your father, who happens to be a "respected" church deacon. (Yes, we have dealt with issues like this and many more too numerous to list.)

*Texas Bible Institute alumni represent
thirty-eight states and thirty-two nations.*

A Bunch of Nuts

November is lovely here in central Texas, with tallow leaves turning red and the crunch of acorn shells sounding underfoot. One day as a noise sounded when I stepped on a nut, God said, "Pick it up." After I reached down for the tiny brown nut, my Teacher asked, "What is it?"

"Lord, this is an acorn," I replied.

"Look again," He suggested.

Three times I insisted that it was an acorn.

Three times He implied, "No."

Wrong? A Texas girl who has spent her life hearing the crunch of acorn shells? Knowing that He would prevail eventually, I humbly asked, "So Lord, if it's not an acorn, what is it?"

"You see an acorn, but I see a mighty oak," He replied. "You see dysfunctional TBI students, but I see world changers."

I never looked at our students the same way again—even though at times they acted like a bunch of nuts! Among the misguided souls were three girls whose poor judgment forced us to place them on disciplinary probation. Their offense? Shoplifting at Walmart. Not only was I disappointed in them, but their lack of remorse also irritated me. The phrase "stuck on stupid" applies here. It was bad enough that rumors about our school being some kind of strange cult or a cover for dangerous "druggies" had already circulated. What would I say to our teachers or the librarian whom I had assured, "These are good kids, not some kind of thugs"?

I rehearsed my own leadership training courses, thinking of my teaching: "When your children or those entrusted into your care make a poor choice, be quick to check the motive. If it was simply immaturity, give them mercy and be assured they will grow up in time. But if it's a lack of character, pounce on it quickly with the appropriate consequence, lest it consume their lives." I knew these girls had displayed bad character. And they weren't sorry, just sorry that they got caught. Anger surging, I could have closed down the school right then. I decided to expel these students and refuse their parents a refund, just for making us the laughing stock of our small town.

Any parent who has watched his offspring make dumb decisions or act in outright defiance can relate to these feelings. I caution anyone currently experiencing this kind of situation to hold off acting on impulse. Instead, pray. Anyone who is filled with the Spirit should expect dreams and visions, especially the John 16:13 type, where He gives you a clear picture. These "eyes of understanding" can confirm or change your intended course. And that day God showed me what an error it would be to expel these three girls.

As I prayed, in my spirit I saw a large hand descend from the sky. It reached for a saltshaker sitting on a nearby table and inverted it. Suddenly the table turned into a world map. As God's mighty hand shook, the shaker poured out TBI alumni across the world.

Some I recognized; others I did not. (This happened in 2001, and we now have thousands of alumni representing Jesus all over the world.) When I returned to the realm of my senses, a fresh awareness of our mandate to disciple young adults gripped my heart. I sensed a new, unconditional love for these students. Four months later they walked across our commencement stage wearing their "Blood of Jesus" red cap and gowns. Thousands applauded their rebound, which occurred slowly through a daily commitment to making good choices.

THE PROCESS OF DISCIPLESHIP

When I was a student nurse, my teachers discipled me in the ways of patient care. An instructor would wrap a leg wound while I watched her every move. Two hours later I would rewrap the wound as my instructor watched. Eventually I performed such tasks myself. You will know your training is complete when a task becomes second nature. Or you find yourself thinking, "Now how would my instructor do this?"

The root word for disciple is *mathetes*, which means to be a follower of a person or doctrine. A philosophy major may be a disciple of Plato or Aristotle; a musician might be a disciple of Ludwig van Beethoven. However, being a disciple of Jesus is much more significant. The men I just mentioned are no longer alive, so their disciples know their teacher only as an historical figure. While they can draw inspiration and influence from them, they can't enjoy a relationship. Disciples of Christ can personally know their Master, who is very much alive. His presence is so addicting and His approval so fulfilling that ten of His original twelve disciples joyfully died as martyrs.

This is the kind of man worth following and learning from. We become His disciples as we draw closer to Him through reading the Word and seeking Him in prayer. This is a lifelong process.

Let's face it; God doesn't wave a magic wand over us at the point of our conversion. Although we become new inside, our outer man remains the same. We still need to grow in God through discipleship. Whether you are a parent, a ministry leader, or part of the daily workforce, God told us to "go therefore and make disciples of all the nations" (Matt. 28:19), with an emphasis on "make." You must be intentional. Your priority as a Christian is to make disciples. With some simple guidance you can do it.

Making disciples is not a task delegated solely to pastors, missionaries, visiting evangelists, or parents. We all should interact with other believers so we can both find the sparks to grow in grace and offer them. Everyone should have a Paul whom you learn from, a Barnabas who holds you accountable, and a Timothy whom you instruct. Have you accepted Jesus's commandment to disciple others, inspire them, and encourage them? Nothing fertilizes your faith as much as discovering that you have eternal influence over someone else.

Discipleship is simple: it is intentionally helping people grow in Christ. This is more than a "Do you need a ride to church?" phone call, although that is a good start. This is "doing life together" so a new convert can watch you respond to a sarcastic waiter or see you joyfully maneuver through rush hour traffic, and learn how to pray using *their* words instead of King James's *thees* and *thous*. Success is helping others achieve spiritual growth. The joy of knowing that you've made a significant deposit in someone's faith will make any other kind of success pale by comparison.

Our Lord taught us why we should disciple. His twelve close followers make a fascinating study. Although He chose a conglomeration of personalities, their love for Him created a mutual affection between them. They were brothers in every sense of the word, including sibling rivalry-like spats, hidden agendas, and ulterior motives. Nevertheless, as they followed Him, He redirected their priorities and purified their motives.

TBI's new four-month programs are a safe place for young adults to mature.

TEACHING VS. TRAINING

There is a distinct difference between teaching and training. A young neurosurgeon might have passed his exam on a craniotomy, but until he performs several, he can't handle surgery. Teaching is for the head; it says, "Know it." Training is for the hands; it says, "Do it." Making a disciple requires both. Someone probably taught you how to ride a bicycle by placing you on the seat and holding the bike in place while you spun the pedals. Disciples need to learn to study God's Word and other daily disciplines to help them develop spiritually. Training is repetitive practice with the objective of accomplishing an end result—over and over, until you can say as Professor Higgins did in *My Fair Lady*, "By George, she's got it!"

The need to shape and instruct reminds me of a rebellious pothos ivy plant I wrestled with not too long ago. The fact that horticulturists have nicknamed it "devil's ivy" should have given me a clue about its uncooperative nature. While I planned to make it climb vertically, the plant set out to grow horizontally. Observing its wayward growth spurts, I inserted a stake into the clay pot and physically wrapped the stem around the stake. Each time I walked past it, I would press the branch and coo to my little rebel, "My plan is greater than your plan. If you'll cooperate with me, it will all make sense in a few months." Over the next week it gradually conformed to the stake, growing ever so obediently upward. Life seemed beautiful until I left my green friend for a four-day journey. When I returned, rebellion had reappeared and my perfect ivy was growing downward. With a chastening chat and gentle redirection, life turned happily upward again.

The Amplified version of Proverbs 22:6 confirms that God designed each of us with a specific gift and bent. Some have a bent toward structure while the adrenaline rush fuels others. Even though we are all wired differently, our daily disciplines assure we are growing upward toward God. They function as my ivy's stake did.

This doesn't mean one can master the Word or following Christ in some kind of simple three-step plan. When Paul wrote the Philippians about His confidence that "He who has begun a good work in you will complete it until the day of Jesus Christ" (Phil. 1:6), the apostle signified that spiritual growth is a lifelong process. Discipleship requires training, which leads to an individual using his or her gifts for the purposes of God. At TBI we wrap twenty-somethings around and around seven basic disciplines to direct their personal development upward. As they form habits, they become beautiful plantings of the Lord.

We teach our students that their daily disciplines will determine their destiny. Super Bowl coaches, classical violinists, and military strategists all know this. Daily drills and repetitive rehearsals produce skills and habits that become second nature, causing their apprentice to kick into autopilot. We need daily disciplines so we won't settle for the easy way out. These disciplines confront and conquer naturally lazy "I don't want to make the effort" inclinations. No person ever became great by doing what he or she pleased.

Daily disciplines develop internal strength and become an anchor for life's oncoming storms. They chisel greatness into our being as they correct, mold, strengthen, and perfect us. Show me someone who has accomplished anything of any significance, and I will show you a disciplined person. Daily disciplines direct your growth. They are the stakes that guide you upward. You are the sum total of what you do daily.

DIVINE DISCIPLINES

Whether you call it habit or discipline, life runs better when you set out with defined plans in place instead of flying by the seat of your pants. We find the root of *disciple* in the word *discipline*. We selected seven disciplines that we found in our studies of the life of Jesus to form the foundations of TBI's training program. Let them guide you in your own call to intentional discipleship. Focus on these three verbs as you develop these holy habits:

- Decide: Something you do with your mind: "I appeal to you therefore, brethren, and beg of you in view of [all] the mercies of God, to make a decisive dedication of your bodies [presenting all your members and faculties] as a living sacrifice, holy (devoted, consecrated) and well pleasing to God" (Rom. 12:1, AMP).

- Discipline: Something you do with your body. First you form your habits and then your habits form you. Daily disciplines become holy habits when dedicated to God.

- Delight: Something you do with your spirit and heart. As you nurture holy habits, "Delight yourself also in the LORD" (Ps. 37:4).

The discipline of prayer

A look at the life of Jesus's life confirms that prayer was the secret to Christ's effectiveness. His disciples clearly connected His prayer life with His power when they said, "Lord, teach us to pray" (Luke 11:1). The discipline of prayer suggests a set time and location. For entrepreneurs and business owners, consider it a key appointment. For girls, whatever your age, consider it a date. For weary mothers, consider it a daily spa. For discouraged ministers, consider it therapy. The key here is to pray daily for at least ten minutes (although you shouldn't get hung up on time or "performance"; besides, the more you pray, the more you will want to pray).

Explain to your disciples that prayer will someday become their favorite time of day and is likely to expand beyond ten minutes. It is exciting to have an audience with the Creator, especially when He is your Father.

Remind younger disciples that prayer is not handing God a "Santa Claus list" and convincing Him they haven't been naughty. It is a two-way exchange of heartfelt communication with an all-knowing, all-loving Father. Some might suggest that a consistent, daily prayer time is legalistic, but once people submit their hearts and schedules to God, prayer becomes a much-needed trip to the living waters. Encourage them to drop the religious lingo and simply talk to the Lord. Train them to listen to Him, to "be still, and know that I am God" (Ps. 46:10). Practicing His presence is just that—practice. I like to rephrase Psalm 23:1 to say: "The Lord is my shepherd; I shall not rush."

Someone may ask if his daily prayer time should be in the morning or at night. In the past I was absurdly legalistic about "starting each day with Jesus." That is, until I married a night owl whose midnight seasons of prayer made me quite jealous. What about you? Do you care what time of the day your children come to enjoy being with you? Neither does the Father. Tell them to just come daily, not because they feel like it or because it is convenient. As with each topic I review in this chapter, daily disciplines will determine their destiny.

The discipline of giving

Those who are discipling others need to teach them to not restrict their giving. Giving includes sharing a smile, a healing hug, a ride home, a favorite recording, or anything else that is an integral part of their life. Learning to give yourself away helps God's children to avoid the worldly practice of self-absorption. This is more important than one might realize because while you can give without loving, you can't love without giving. I have noticed visitors at our church squirm nervously when we announce that Believers World Outreach Church observes four offerings at every service. That is, until we explain that we first give (offer) our praise to God in song, then give (offer) God's love to one another, give (offer) honor to God's Word and the role of our pastor, and, finally, give (offer) our finances.

Concerning finances, Paul instructs us to give to those who minister the gospel (1 Cor. 9:7) and on a weekly basis (1 Cor. 16:1–2). Make intentional, disciplined giving a part of your planned budget—in contrast to spontaneous, Holy Spirit–led "goose bump" offerings, even though the latter are precious. Some believers vow to give something at every offering, even if it's only a nickel, as a visible sign of their gratitude. Inspire your disciples to give daily in order to cultivate a spirit of generosity.

The discipline of fasting

Fasting is voluntary abstinence from a substance. Although many define this as food, you can fast from most anything—be it a habit, practice, hobby, or physical pleasure—for the purpose of growing spiritually. Fasting is an act of worship and obedience. It is a powerful secret for personal victory and a weapon of spiritual warfare. In Jesus's legendary Sermon on the Mount He twice referred to the practice with the comment "*When* you fast..." (Matt. 6:16–17, emphasis added), not "*If* you fast..." The Bible records nine types of fasts, but those are for a specific purpose and different from what Jesus taught about.

An example of this discipline could involve skipping lunch every Tuesday or abstaining from dessert on Fridays. As you and your disciples grow in the discipline of fasting, consider offering an entire day as an act of worship. Some people ask, "Rachel, do you see visions when you fast?" Joking, I respond, "Yes, I certainly do. I see visions of pizza and blueberry pancakes." At first, fasting may prove difficult, but reassure them that ultimately they will experience personal victory and grow so spiritually attuned to God that they will see its value. Challenge them to fast from something daily. That could be carnal joking, a second helping at dinner, or a whiny response.

The discipline of Bible reading

Daily Bible reading is the single greatest discipline you can help someone develop, since it offers unlimited rewards. The Bible is a book about a Father and His family and a love letter to His children. You can learn about everything He desires for you, including paths to success and warnings to the wise in His Word. It is progressive, unfolding revelation of God and His unconditional love and an invitation to enjoy benefits purchased by the blood of Jesus, which created His new covenant with man. John 1:1 says, "In the beginning was the Word, and the Word was with God, and the Word was God." Since Jesus is the Word, we fellowship with Him through the Word, and He communicates to us through it. While people talk to God in prayer, in Bible reading God talks to them.

As with prayer, your objective is to assist disciples in creating a designated time and place for Bible reading and study so they can develop a disciplined habit. Suggest starting with one chapter or a single psalm. Train them to read the Word slowly and prayerfully, recognizing that the Bible is a love letter from their Father. We teach TBI students three ways they can enjoy the Bible, each of them beneficial. Colleagues laugh at my "simplistic" descriptions, but decades later they still remember them. They are the bird, frog, and caterpillar approaches.

The bird approach provides a panoramic overview, causing you to soar over its content for the purpose of getting the big picture and understanding the Bible as a whole. Read three chapters each day, and you will cover the Bible in one year.

The frog approach, also known as devotional reading, is comfort food at its best. Hopping from one favorite scripture to another keeps you strong.

The caterpillar approach involves systematic study, focusing (or chewing) on a small portion.

Whatever method they use, give your disciples three challenges:

1. Read the Bible as if it were a love letter from your Father.

2. Enjoy what you understand and put the more difficult portions on the proverbial shelf.

3. As you read, ask the Holy Spirit questions and wait quietly.

Also, tell them the tutor known as the Holy Spirit will often answer questions by bringing another scripture to mind. What other book talks back to the reader? However, I would make a distinction between devotional reading and study. Devotional reading fills your heart; studying fills your head. The only thing worse than an empty-headed believer is a religious intellectual, so encourage *both* types of reading.

Free parental advice

By reading well-known Bible stories repetitively, parents can develop in their children the habit of daily Bible time. When ours were young, we acted out bedtime stories so vividly that one night Andrew asked if he needed to clean Goliath's blood off of the carpet before they went to sleep. Keep it short so they look forward to it. Generally age is equivalent to attention span, so a six-year-old should hear a six-minute story. By the time kids turn eight, I suggest they read a chapter per day with you. By ten insist they read it themselves.

Will this be easy? Not at all. By bedtime I often felt so exhausted with the duties of raising three youngsters amid the rest of my to-do list that I started tossing things overboard (the duties, not the kids). Quite often I could choose to help them read their Bible *or* brush their teeth. When I had to choose between the two, I spent my last ounce of energy reading some verses. By their teens I was thankful that I helped them hide God's Word in their hearts—and that their teeth survived.

The discipline of serving

Serving is the core of Christianity. As Mother Teresa once said, "If you can't feed one hundred people, feed one."[1] The motive of genuine serving is to help people without expecting anything in return. Although it is true that what you do in secret God will reward openly, I find it precious to serve simply out of a heart of love. Some people think that serving is to "do it heartily, as to the Lord and not to men" (Col. 3:23), but I believe we should go a notch higher. Serving should be fueled by a genuine love for another person, place, or nation. Often people grumble, "Well, this is not my idea of a great weekend, but I'm doing it for Jesus." We should inspire those we intentionally disciple to do something for someone daily, just because in God's eyes all people are valuable. We should do it as a daily discipline.

The discipline of a strong work ethic

God bless the parents who take time to teach their children how to work diligently. Over the years at our Discovery Camps we have employed twenty-five hundred young adults, all of them TBI alumni. It only takes a few days to discern who comes from hard-working stock. For those who didn't learn at home, we show them this scripture: "Work willingly at whatever you do, as though you were working for the Lord rather than for people. Remember that the Lord will give you an inheritance as your reward, and that the Master you are serving is Christ" (Col. 3:23–24, NLT).

Many employers have sent us letters to commend the work ethic of TBI graduates. We tell all our students, "Start with a smile and end with a song. Arrive early and stay a few minutes late. Be quick to send your employer a thank-you note, and absolutely refuse to dishonor him with complaining or gossip." Not that everyone responds to that perfectly. Sometimes a staff member oversleeps or doesn't even show up for work, whining, "I'm tired." To which we respond: "So what? We have twelve hundred guests who deserve breakfast. Get to work, please."

One day a dear staffer said, "I don't want to work today. My job is too hard." I responded, "Compared to whom? The single moms who work two jobs to responsibly pay their bills? Our wounded veterans?" Although I gave him my famous "Toughen up, Buttercup" speech, I also slipped him his favorite candy bar that night. Developing a strong work ethic takes time, but don't allow people to wimp out. Being a Christian is not an excuse for laziness; it should represent an incentive to represent Him. Paul worked many hours a day as a tentmaker to avoid being a financial burden to others. What a great example! Train your disciples to work daily, reminding them that the Word of God has many scriptures about diligence, such as:

+ "He who has a slack hand becomes poor, but the hand of the diligent makes rich" (Prov. 10:4).

+ "The hand of the diligent will rule, but the lazy man will be put to forced labor" (Prov. 12:24).

+ "The soul of a lazy man desires, and has nothing; but the soul of the diligent shall be made rich" (Prov. 13:4).

+ "Do you see a man who excels in his work? He will stand before kings; he will not stand before unknown men" (Prov. 22:29).

+ "She watches over the ways of her household, and does not eat the bread of idleness" (Prov. 31:27).

The discipline of rest and recreation

The American Dream has helped create some self-centered, over-achieving workaholics who push themselves far beyond healthy boundaries. Those who finally win the rat race accomplish nothing other than becoming the chief rat. Friends who are passionate about ministry are not far behind those in the rat race—including Tommy and me. After all, there is always one more call to make or one more letter to write. Small wonder, then, that a third of Americans are sleep-deprived, which causes them to have problems with memory or depression and weakens their immune system. Sleep-deprived people tested on a driving simulator or performing hand-eye coordination tasks perform as badly, or worse, than those who are intoxicated. According to the National Highway Traffic Safety administration, 1,550 motor vehicle deaths a year are due to sleep-deficient drivers.[2]

Stress is an American epidemic depleting our physical and mental resources. Jesus attempted to set boundaries for us when He said, "For you have the poor with you always [demands and pressures clamoring for your attention], but Me you do not have always. For in pouring this fragrant oil on My body, she did it for My burial. Assuredly, I say to you, wherever this gospel is preached in the whole world, what this woman has done will also be told as a memorial to her" (Matt. 26:11–13). Through this, Jesus wasn't telling us to neglect the poor, but to recognize His presence as our number-one priority.

If we were only a spirit being, we would never need to stop. However, our physical bodies and emotional wholeness demand it. Just as a bird needs both wings to balance it in flight, humans need work and play to remain whole. If we don't take time to come apart, we will eventually fall apart. Hobbies, exercise, and recreation help recharge our batteries. Rest and play daily, conscious that you are serving as an example. Let those you are discipling see you have fun and enjoy life.

WORKS OR GRACE?

Are these seven daily disciplines learned behavior or a work of the Spirit? Works or grace? Will they produce a disciple of Jesus Christ with a life-giving heart or a Pharisee who is impressed with his "religious black belts"? It depends whether the person is communing with her Creator or simply completing a checklist. Train disciples to know the difference between daily disciplines and promptings of the Holy Spirit. The daily disciplines are for their character, and the latter are for all the other characters. Developing daily disciplines will assure our private lives are as strong as our public lives, which is an overflow of the first.

CUTTING OFF EARS

Despite our passion to make balanced disciples at TBI, we have seen some "cut off ears," a phrase originating with Matthew 26:51, where a zealous Peter cut off the high priest's servant's ear in the Garden of Gethsemane. Can you imagine Jesus rolling His eyes and glaring at Peter as He bends to the ground to retrieve the bloody blob and offering an apologetic, "Sorry 'bout that; he's still learning" comment before placing it back on the man's head? Face it: disciples are learners who make mistakes, have misdirected zeal, and break rules, all "in the name of the Lord."

Two of our zealous sons in the Lord once marched into a hospital to pray for people, boldly telling a startled patient, "We've come to heal you." The senior citizen answered, "Well, I'll take the prayer but not sure if it will work because I have COPD." Said one of the students, "I don't know what COPD is, but we have J-E-S-U-S."

Another time we challenged young people to bring an offering for the church's building fund, promising the winner an award. Stunned by a boy's two-hundred-dollar offering, we asked, "How did you raise so much money?"

"Oh, it was simple," he replied. "The Lord gave me a great idea."

We later learned that while people were in church, he stole several hubcaps and sold them. We had to explain to him that that idea wasn't from the Lord.

TBI's Prayer Culture

At TBI we have taught classes on prayer and required devotional prayer time, but neither had the impact of a student-led movement called "Prayer Culture." As a teen, our second-oldest son, Peter, felt called to a life of intercession. God had confirmed that to me in a dream, which I held in my heart for six years. In this dream I saw the back of an exhausted preteen, attempting to cut eighty-five acres with a push mower. Compassion flooded my heart over the immensity of the task—and the child's steadfastness. When he turned toward me, I realized it was Peter. In the dream I cried out, "Oh, God, help him. Bring out the big boys!" Then, from across the vast acreage, I saw huge combines coming up out of the ground—first one, then three, and then six and ten. Peter flashed his famous grin and the harvest began. When I awakened, I knew instantly that God had called Peter as an intercessor.

When Peter and his buddy committed their lives to Spirit-led prayer, it sparked miracles. One spark erupted into a fire of revival, resulting in sixteen weekly online connections of passionate worship and intercession. Youth groups gather in living rooms while alumni watch and pray across the world. Sometimes it is a time of gentle prayer; other times it is quite a pep rally. We don't struggle with getting students to pray anymore; we often must make them quit so they can go to bed. Instead of the typical pre-graduation pranks, in April 2011 our dynamic Prayer Culture team hosted twenty-four hours of prayer in one-hour allotments. The presence of God shook us to the core. These young people were so lit up that I momentarily felt sorry for the devil. They know too much, and he has no chance.

TIME-RELEASE MIRACLES

Whether it is our beautiful students or your grandchildren, making disciples is not instantaneous. I liken it to time-release capsules that will provide them what they need throughout their day, year, or life. At the most unexpected moments you will receive a miracle testimony from someone in your past. That seed of guidance that you planted produced a Christ-exalting adult. Such is the personal joy of having sons and daughters in the Lord. As we all make discipleship the priority that Jesus intended, we will see miracle moments, shaken out like huge saltshakers around the world. I close with what I call the "Seven Holy Habits."

Learn to pray a little each day (prayer).
Then ask, "What does the Word say?" (Bible reading).
Learn to fast, but not too fast (fasting).
Learn to play, so you will last (rest and recreation).
Serving others puts them first (serving).

A heart to give heals many hurts (giving).
Learn to work and not to shirk (work).
Holy habits give life a perk (rewards).

I dedicate those "Seven Holy Habits" to the young champions at Believers World Outreach Church.

THE MIRACLE OF DISCIPLESHIP

What our Lord said about cross-bearing and obedience is not in fine type. It is in bold print on the face of the contract.

—Vance Havner[3]

He is no fool who gives what he cannot keep, to gain what he cannot lose.

—Jim Elliott, martyred missionary[4]

Disciples are made not born.

—Walter A. Henrichsen[5]

The dictionary is the only place where success comes before hard work.

—Vince Lombardi[6]

CHAPTER 11

God's Plan Is Family

ે Life Question: What is God's plan for my family?

ે Miracle Moment: The miracle of family

ે Life Lesson: Seasons are for seasoning.

ONE DAY AS I JUGGLED MULTIPLE RESPONSIBILITIES, THE WEIGHT of societal expectations placed on women in the modern era caved in on me. However, in that instant I suddenly felt peace flooding my spirit as God spoke to me: "You can have it all, but you can't have it all at the same time."

A fulfilling, lifelong marriage and producing a Christ-centered family is the most admirable goal a man and woman can achieve. As legendary English scholar and writer C. S. Lewis one said, "The homemaker has the ultimate career."[1] God's plan is the family. Period. The Bible is all about God the Father and His family. Before a church, a school, or a business existed, God established the family. And before the family, He arranged marriage.

I want to share a poem the Lord gave me about life's changing seasons.

SEASONS ARE FOR SEASONING

Young and zealous, I began to carry out the Master's plan,
An insatiable hunger for His best, until I knew, I would
    not rest.

"Tis the season to get full, so Satan's plan you can annul,
From your Bible you shall learn and never miss My
slightest turn."

I lived in prayer and slept with tapes, I fasted food and
turned down dates.
God's Word grew strong inside of me, God's plan I then
began to see.
'Tis the season to empty out and teach the people all about
His promises in the Word of God, from state to state, I
traveled abroad.

The fruit was pure, the miracles strong, from "glory to
glory" for seven years long.
But in my spirit, the question was raised, "Are you ready
yet for another phase?"
The season changed again in my life, as God honored me
to be Tommy's wife.
I then began to understand the beauty of the Master's
plan.

From cleaning to cooking, great dreams I forsook,
"Lord, are You certain this part's in Your Book?
Just being a servant, a help to this man?
This detour was not exactly a part of my plan."
Because I was selfish, this season was tough.
Enjoy doing laundry? Enough is enough!
But serving God in times that are dull
Makes shade-growing fruit in our life ripe and full.

Slowly and surely God's whisper came through,
"There's many more seasons I must work into you."
What else could there be?

My emotions went hyper as glory to glory turned diaper
    to diaper!
First Andrew, then Peter, and right behind, Abby,
This season called "Mama" has made me so happy.
Each season is different, but purpose abides,
"I know what I'm doing," the Lord gently chides.
"I'm seasoning you so that you'll never care for glamour or
    fame,
You'll be made aware of things that I value, of life from
    My view.
Oh please, won't you grow and let Jesus shine through?"

A season of courage, a season of grace, a caregiver's chair
    in a sad, lonely place.
A season of standing and believing Your Word,
Rejoicing when Daddy's salvation was heard.
A season that's filled with Crayolas and tears,
Of comforting toddlers with irrational fears.
Our kids are now grown and Tommy? Sheer bliss.
This season is fun as we cuddle and kiss.
Reconnecting with him, my amazing man,
A joyful part of this master plan.
Dear Lord, through each season I want You to grow Your
    purpose in me,
So this whole world will know that
Your love is real and Your plan is so great,
You'll fulfill every dream if we'll just learn to wait.

               —Rachel Burchfield

Marriage Matters

Marriage is not a 50-50 contract with a human but a 100 percent covenant with God. While it is tempting to spend more time preparing for the wedding than the marriage, the Word of God has much to say about this subject. A husband has the tall order of loving his wife as Christ loved the church while wives are to honor his leadership. Submission is vastly misunderstood, but from one who has lived it, I assure you that a woman who is loved in the same way Christ loves the church finds submission a joy. Not so the world. Here is how I would describe some differing perspectives on marriage:

- The *Let's Make a Deal* marriage: You thought you found the ideal. Then you learned you got a raw deal, so now you want a new deal.

- The *Flintstones* marriage: Trying to arrive in your own power.

- Consumer-oriented marriage: As long as my spouse meets my needs, I stay. If the costs go up or the rewards go down, I bolt, just as I will if a better alternative comes along.

- Blind marriage: When love at first sight is not enough to hold you over to love at last sight.

- Secular mind-set: They date to marry. I do. I did. I'm done.

- Christian mind-set: They marry to date. I do. I did. It's fun.

I enjoyed a happy childhood. Although my parents were not yet born again, they modeled a morally strong home. Mama was a trailblazing flight attendant, covering a million miles, and then at the age of thirty she married my pilot-father. They had three daughters; I'm the baby. Daddy possessed a strong personality, impressive work ethic, and great sense of humor. I was also blessed with two wonderful sisters. When Daddy was due home from work, Mama would

change out of her day clothes and put on a dress and fresh red lipstick. Daddy paid the bills and maintained the house, while Mama
raised us girls and created a home. We live in a much different world
today, but the principles of preferring each other remain the same.

MY HONG KONG PRAYER

Finishing up a 1982 ministry trip to the Philippine Islands, our
team stayed at the lovely Shangri-La Hotel in Hong Kong. There,
encountering loneliness for the first time in life, I prayed, "Lord, I'm
almost twenty-five years old. I've been so in love with You that I
forgot to get married. I've reduced my list to just three items, please."
(I'm not sure if I no longer cared about the other items, or if I felt
that it would be tougher for Jesus to find Mr. Right than I originally
thought.) This was my list:

1. Please let him be a man of prayer.

2. Let him desire to do a big work for You.

3. If You don't mind and it doesn't change any major part
    of Your eternal plan, please let him have a hairy chest.

As usual the Lord was a step ahead of me. Two months earlier I had met Tommy at a Pizza Hut in Houston. Youth from his
thriving group surrounded him; I also was with a group of teens who
had just returned from a ministry trip to South Texas. Prodded by
his aunt, Tommy came over for a casual "hello," and we exchanged
chitchat. As I reached over the table to get a pitcher of Coke, he
noticed the name "Tommy" across my back pocket. His buddy said,
"Hey! Look at Rachel's jeans. It's prophetic."

The next month Tommy invited me to speak to his youth group.
I accepted. After I ministered a word under a powerful anointing, I
turned the service back to him. Instead of singing my praises, though,
he said, "Well, that was wonderful, but what the Lord is wanting to

do now is blah-blah-blah." Then he opened the altar. I felt rather offended—I was accustomed to people applauding me. Still, I had to admit that a lot of good ministry took place. As he took me home, he asked to pray for my next ministry trip. I thought he just wanted to hold my hand, but the power of God filled his '76 Corvette.

As I trembled walking into my home, I thought, "Wow, that guy can sure pray." Instantly the first item on my checklist popped into my head. A few weeks later he told me, "God called me into ministry as a seven-year-old Mississippi boy, and whether man notices or not, I plan to do something big for Him." Bingo! Item number two. I choked on my coffee as I thought, "What will I do if God really heard my prayer?"

A HAIRY CHEST

Fresh from an amazing time of ministry in Missouri, I heard the phone ringing as I unlocked the front door, suitcase in tow. When I answered, I heard that southern Mississippi accent that by now made my heart skip a few beats: "Raaa-chul, I know that you're just getting home, but I'm taking my youth group to the beach. Wanna come?" I soon found myself in his white Corvette, wondering about request number three. How foolish and carnal I felt to even care about something so trivial. Yet I kept wondering, "What if God really heard me?" Though Galveston Bay wasn't too pretty, I had other things in mind as we parked and prepared to swim. It seemed as though he took off his T-shirt in slow motion; I strained to glance out of the corner of my eyes so I wouldn't appear overly interested. "Hallelujah! Mine eyes had seen the glory!" I thought, "Three out of three, bucko. You're it."

Tommy did far more than meet my three-item checklist. Jesus used him to expose how the Christian celebrity scene was luring me into its trap. "Rachel," he gently said one time, "you might be powerfully used to bless others, but what about you? When the

anointing lifts, you'll still go into a lonely hotel room." Eleven
months later he proposed to me as we stood behind the pulpit
at his church. That probably doesn't sound too romantic, but I
couldn't think of anything more wonderful. We had a storybook
wedding on March 12, 1983.

EARLY MARITAL TENSION

I felt confused. How could I love Tommy so deeply yet be so
annoyed? Although the kindest, most giving man I had ever met,
his big-hearted leadership style clashed with my inclusive, organized
systems. Clearly it was me who needed to grow.

During our first year together two key lessons shaped our marriage. After one angry exchange of words, he packed an overnight
bag and shouted, "I'll be back tomorrow, but I'm leaving tonight." As
he stomped toward the front door, he suddenly yelled, "No!" Then
he threw down his bag and turned back, embraced me passionately
and shouted, "Satan, you won't have our marriage!" I melted into a
puddle of tears. Instead of turning against each other, we learned to
pull together.

Still, we experienced another setback a few months later. I ada-
mantly disagreed with something he planned to do (today I can't
even remember what). As he sat on our gold, Aztec-designed couch,
I stood next to him drinking a Texas-size glass of water. Irritated by
something he said, I poured the entire glass of water on his head. But
before the water hit the floor, I fell to my knees, saying, "I'm sorry,
Tommy. I'm sorry, Jesus." Again, his big strong arms embraced me,
and I heard him pray, "Lord, make me a better husband." I knew
just how David must have felt when he cut King Saul's robe (1 Sam.
24:1–5).

Any act of humility will usually prevent a marital collision. By
preferring one another, we allow Christ's love to become the glue that
bonds us. Marriage is more about doing what is right than deciding

who is right. The spiritually mature individual humbles himself (or herself) first. The late Ruth Bell Graham once said, "A good marriage is the union of two good forgivers."[2] Since human love and emotion quickly fade, learn what the Bible says about God's love—its description, source, and how to activate it. During every tense moment, learn to think, "God's love can fix this." Here are some of my favorite scriptures to strengthen your marriage:

- "A soft answer turns away wrath, but a harsh word stirs up anger" (Prov. 15:1).

- "It is honorable for a man to stop striving, since any fool can start a quarrel" (Prov. 20:3).

- "Love is patient and kind. Love is not jealous or boastful or proud or rude. It does not demand its own way. It is not irritable, and it keeps no record of being wronged" (1 Cor. 13:4–5, NLT).

Check the Amplified Bible's translation of Ephesians 5:33 to see the twelve verbs describing the wife's correct response to her husband. Words such as *admire*, *respect*, and *reverence* make sense, but I particularly like its instruction, *"notices him."* I see far too many a modern wife who is guilty of neglecting her husband and then wonder why he falls in love with his secretary.

You may have heard this elsewhere, but it bears repeating: men and women are wired differently. A basic foundation of a fulfilling marriage is appreciating that men need respect while women crave affection. Husbands, the Bible instructs you to give your wife understanding and honor so that your prayers are not hindered (1 Pet. 3:7). Couples have different ways of doing things. Neither spouse is wrong, just different. Tommy and I are different in many ways. He's tall, and I'm short. He's a night owl, and I'm an early bird. He likes a house full of noise, and I need it peacefully quiet. He unwinds by talking to people on the phone and me by walking and piddling. He is like a hibernating bear, hunkering down with books in his big, blue chair while I love the outdoors. So what?

MARRIAGE SEMINAR

Here is an amusing story about a couple who had been married for nine years. A friend advised Rob and Sharon to attend a marriage seminar to improve their communication skills. The very idea irritated Rob, who prided himself on being an attentive husband. Nevertheless, he agreed. That weekend when the instructor began, "Today we will focus on communication between a man and woman," Rob rolled his eyes. Then the speaker continued, "It is essential that you are attentive to your spouse's likes and dislikes. Men, can you name your wife's favorite flower?" Leaning over and touching his wife's arm, Rob whispered, "It's Pillsbury, isn't it?"

My advice to husbands is to be steadfast in God, chivalrous, and affectionate to your wife in front of your children. If she works outside the home, help her with the housework. Women, you *must* emotionally leave your parents, live within your budget, stay attractive physically, make your home a castle, and keep your sex life fresh. It helps to memorize Psalm 62:5, which talks about waiting on God. As you do, release your spouse from the impossible responsibility of fulfilling your every whim. If you let God be God and your husband your earthly partner, it will prove an unbeatable combination.

When Tommy has been out of town for a few days, my heart beats faster when I know that he's coming home. We have learned that even when you love each other deeply, marriage is still work. A godly, fun, fulfilling marriage is an astounding sign and wonder in today's fragmented, divorce-plagued society. I dare you to go for it.

What Is a Family?

A family is a safe incubator that nurtures strength, creativity, and emotional wholeness. God designed the family to provide acceptance, affirmation, relational instruction, and tools for successful living. Unity and diversity, form and freedom, and togetherness and individuality are all shaped by the family. We belong to one another, are affected by one another, feel compassion and concern for one another, and are interested in one another. While we never remain static in life, family is where our story begins. We who were raised in a loving home should be quick to reach out to those who were not. No one should go through life alone.

The urban expression, "I've got your back," is keenly descriptive of God's idea of family. Ecclesiastes describes more than two dozen of life's experiences that are common to all: "a time to be born, and a time to die...a time to laugh; a time to mourn" (Eccles. 3:2, 4). Why family? Because life is so fragile and unpredictable. God intended for the family to provide vital support for each member. God wants you to enjoy your family socially and strengthen each member spiritually.

Now if family is God's idea, why are so many families in such a mess? Sin and selfishness. A broken relationship confirms the failure to meet an emotional need. It takes patience to build relationships by listening to someone's laundry list of complaints and disappointments, or investing time in things others enjoy. It can be far more convenient to rush out the door to do your own thing than confront your selfishness. It doesn't take much neglect for a home to become a hotel where members ignore the other guests. If your family members are not enjoying supportive, transparent, two-sided friendships with one another, it is high time for an evaluation. As Christians we should commit to be accessible and open to family members who need prayer or a friend. Strong family relationships prove that your Christianity is authentic. If it doesn't work at home, don't export it.

Tools and Rules

Setting down rules for children without a loving relationship breeds rebellion, just as relationships without rules breed anarchy. Families need structure built around God's unconditional love. Anything less leads to insecurity and dysfunction. Constantly reinforce the mantra, "We are family and this is what families do." If parents nurture kindness, honor, and diligence in their children, other issues tend to work themselves out. If you provide tools along with rules, friendships within the family will flourish. For example, how should siblings deal with jealousy? Is privacy permissible? What are the consequences of lying to your parents? Every day should include affirming words on making good choices. I believe in providing direction more than correction.

Setting ground rules with such catchphrases as "kindness is king" and "always do your best" will provide a target. These two rules apply to everything from sarcasm and sibling rivalry to cleaning the bathroom and paying bills. The family needs to feature patience for immaturity and a long fuse for unsettled issues. Don't just spout rules; give children tools. It is within the accepting atmosphere of a family that a child learns how to appropriately deal with anger and a teen learns to control incessant complaining. Much of this is caught, not taught. Children learn honor when Mom greets Dad at the door with a fresh glass of iced tea, or a child watches their older sibling mow the yard without being told.

The Extended Family

The longer I'm alive, the more I believe in the three-generational family dynamic. The older members need the energy of the young while the young need the wisdom of the old. A family reunion is a good portrait of God's plan for extended family. Do you see that newborn cradled in a grandmother's arms? Women swapping recipes? Men swapping websites? Do you see that patient grandfather trapped in a corner chair by his geeky grandson, who is excited about his newest tech toy? That's family.

God's tri-generational family plan appears in the Abraham-Isaac-Jacob paradigm. Jacob was fifteen years old when his famous grandfather "breathed his last and died, and was gathered to his people" (Gen. 35:29). We can be certain that Jacob heard Grandpa Abraham's stories sitting around a dancing fire in the Sinai desert. First came Abraham's version of sacrificing Isaac on the altar; then came Isaac's version. We can assume that Grandpa Abe's stories of that unexpected visit by "Melchizedek, the mystery man," and the Promised Land filled many a boring night. The children might have rolled their eyes: "Uh, Gramps, we've heard that story before." Don't think so? How many times did your grandfather tell his favorite football or fishing story?

Jesus said, "For what profit is it to a man if he gains the whole world, and loses his own soul? Or what will a man give in exchange for his soul?" (Matt. 16:26). I feel the same way about family. What have we accomplished if we win the world but lose our marriage and family? There is no sacrifice too great to keep your marriage and family intact. However, if you have already experienced the pain of divorce, don't try to unscramble those eggs. Give them to God and let Him create an omelet just for you.

After all, many TBI students come from broken homes but still lead full lives. Following are some comments they expressed in a survey of six hundred students. By the way, 50 percent of the respondents mentioned how they secretly appreciated parental accountability during their teen years. And 80 percent talked about how much they valued family meals, church involvement, and holiday traditions.

+ "Grandma knit each of us a sweater when we graduated from elementary school."

+ "Dad served us family Communion before a new school year and on New Year's Day."

+ "If my words hurt my sibling, I had to clean his bathroom. Anger management!"

+ "My mom didn't preach to my friends. Her famous fettuccine won them over."

+ "Grandpa taught me how to bait a hook, scale a fish, and throw a football."

+ "Before it leaked out, Dad asked for our forgiveness over his adultery."

+ "I knew that Dad was going to check my computer and cell phone every month."

+ "My uncle took us camping each summer since we didn't have a dad anymore."

+ "Mama refused to criticize my father's new wife, which made my visits easier."

+ "During meals Mom blared Christian rock just to introduce me to it."

+ "Each month Grandma taught me how to scrapbook, and I taught her video games."

+ "Every Friday was family night; we played board games and watched movies, and one friend was allowed to join us."

+ "Once we agreed on a church home, missing Sunday service was not an option."

+ "When I was twelve, Mama and I hosted a spring tea
   party, which is now a tradition."

THE FAMILY OF GOD

The church is God's blueprint for a family. No father would put
his newborn on a street corner and walk away. Likewise, when you
became a child of God, your Father placed you into a church to
learn how His family is to act. At church you learn His ways from
loving brothers and sisters in Christ. Your spiritual growth, emotional well-being, and sense of purpose are directly connected to
your commitment to a healthy congregation.

Those who lack the support of a natural family especially need
the strength of God's family. As Psalm 68:6 says: "God sets the
solitary in families." That can apply to singles, the divorced or wid-
owed, military families—the list goes on and on. Recently I watched
a foster child crying in the arms of a World War II veteran before
they prayed. An hour later they were laughing together at a sandwich shop. That's the church in action. Healthy churches have
leaders who are growing, accountable, and accessible. They inspire
you to be "planted in the house of the LORD" (Ps. 92:13) so—as the
latter part of the verse says—you will flourish.

Given God's affirmation of the church, I find it inconceivable
how many believers are not committed to a church, instead hopping
around from place to place. There are several reasons to avoid this
habit:

First, it promotes a restaurant mentality: "What do I want to
eat today?"

Instead of serving others, it places an emphasis on getting
blessed and a "what's in it for me?" mentality while preventing the
growth of healthy relationships.

Church hoppers have a lack of accountability to a pastoral team,
which reveals a lack of character and an unteachable spirit.

Such fickleness disqualifies a person from leadership.

Besides, frequently changing churches is as foolish as changing families every time your mom made meat loaf or your brother picked a fight. Don't blow up; grow up.

RAISING GODLY CHILDREN

Raising children to love God, love one another, and love life is a full-time task. Put aside any competing priorities for another season. At the time of this writing, our three children are in their twenties and demonstrate a vibrant relationship with Jesus and a deep love for one another. They are in leadership positions in ministry, and we couldn't be prouder. Forgive my constant references to them, but they validate my child-rearing principles. People are constantly asking me, "What was your secret to raising such great kids?" It's no secret; I tell everyone who will listen.

It starts with intentional salvation. Your primary objective is introducing them to a loving God. As they learn who He is, they will comprehend that they are His masterpiece, created for His pleasure. Meditate on these three Judeo-Christian concepts from Psalm 127:3–4. Children are: 1) a blessing, 2) a reward, and 3) arrows that need sharpening and purpose. When they are toddlers, tell them often, "You are such a blessing and God's reward to me." Parents can describe the person of Jesus so delightfully that children will accept Him as Savior at a young age. For example, when they see another child crying at the park, you can whisper, "If Jesus were here, He would comfort that child." When reading a bedtime story about Esther, you can nonchalantly say, "Someday soon you'll probably invite this Jesus into your heart and He'll guide you, just like He's guiding Esther in this story."

Andrew was three when we played the old "knock, knock" game on Christmas Eve. At the end I explained that Jesus was knocking on his heart, so he invited Jesus to live in his heart forever. He vividly remembers the experience. Peter was five when he said, "A blue puppet told me to give my heart to Jesus, so I did." Abby got saved in the backseat of our car because Andrew promised her a cool, star-studded certificate. I suggest that you make a huge deal celebrating such occasions. Consider hosting a spontaneous birthday party to celebrate "the new you." It will help them understand the significance of their decision. Explain from that moment on, they will be loved and guided by their inner man. Yes, even a five-year-old!

Our junior staff, ready to help
(from left) Peter, Andrew, and Abby

THREE SUBLIMINAL MESSAGES

Parents send multiple self-image-forming messages to toddlers, many of them silent. Here are three that will assist their emotional development.

One of the most important messages you can send is, "You are accepted," a concept rooted in unconditional love.

Parents who always apologize for a child's behavior, fashion choices, or performance are sending a subliminal message the youngster interprets as: "I'm not good enough." Our children grew up in the proverbial fishbowl—on the Discovery Camp stage. Andrew proved a charming child, singing difficult solos and wowing crowds at the age of three. Unlike his "perfect" brother, at three Peter stuck his tongue out at our guests (everyone except me laughed). Annoyed by his foolishness, I felt embarrassed that he did not behave like Andrew. Once, just as I prepared to compare him to Andrew before correcting him, the Holy Spirit gave me an idea: accept him! So, as I hugged him I said, "Peter, I am so proud of you. God has given you a gift to make people laugh, and you did a good job of that today. Next time let's use that gift to make people happy instead of making them feel unloved. Let me know what ideas the Lord gives you, OK?" Peter's humor and creativity have since blessed tens of thousands of campers. I am grateful that the Holy Spirit redirected my parental approach.

Frequently tell your child, "You are needed."

Busy parents feel tempted to shove their children into a corner so they can do things that seem more important. When video games and TV become babysitters at an early age, children grow up thinking they are in the way. *Children should never feel as though they are an interruption.* I intentionally created simple, age-appropriate tasks to let our children know they were needed. During the summer I prepared them for Miracle Rallies, telling them, "Daddy and Mama are going to help campers receive the love of Jesus tonight, and we need you to help us." As a three-year-old, Abby was the only one small enough to weave through packed altars, passing out Kleenex to sobbing campers. I wanted to nurture the compassion that I recognized in her.

Meanwhile, high-energy Peter possessed an all-consuming need for adventure. At the age of ten he spent hours zooming across our pasture on his bright yellow four-wheeler. So I commissioned him to make a large "Welcome" flag. When ladies arrived for my "Women In Leadership" retreats, he and Abby were eager and prepared to help. I stationed our sweet daughter at the front barricade to welcome pastor's wives with candy, while Peter and I raced incoming cars on his four-wheeler. What a hilarious picture. While his "Welcome" flag and Mom were both hanging on for dear life, he felt very important.

The third message to instill in children is: "You are unique."

Find something that distinguishes them from others and celebrate it. Accomplishments breed self-confidence, so by the time they start elementary school, help them to master something. I particularly like the way the Amplified Bible phrases Proverbs 22:6: "Train up a child in the way he should go [and in keeping with his individual gift or bent], and when he is old he will not depart from it." Whether it is creativity, athletics, fine arts, or literature, every child has a bent. When we played the *Memory* board game, nine-year-old Abby smeared me. I easily recognized her intellectual bent. At twenty-one she earned the right to study abroad at Oxford University through a Baylor University program. God deposited gifts in your child at conception. Nurture them throughout their childhood.

Abby + children = destiny

SPIRITUAL TRAINING

Parents who make time to teach and train their children in spiritual matters will reap a lifetime of rewards. While teaching puts good things in their heads, training requires them to practice. No parenting expert can compete with Deuteronomy's parental challenge: "And these words which I command you today shall be in your heart. You shall teach them diligently to your children, and shall talk of them when you sit in your house, when you walk by the way, when you lie down, and when you rise up" (Deut. 6:6–7). Incidentally this puts the sole responsibility of teaching children about God on parents, not pastors. I'm not endorsing a rigid lifestyle of following religious rules, but a natural overflow of your walk with Jesus.

One the greatest ideas I heard comes from a wonderful couple who served with us for many years. Before their toddlers went to sleep, their parents instructed them to kiss the Bible, which left an indelible mark on these children. This is creative parenting at its best. I believe the Holy Spirit will give you unique ideas to imprint God's Word into their hearts, regardless of age.

One afternoon Peter and I played together in his tree house, collecting crab apples for ammunition against imaginary pirates. Although we stockpiled about twenty in the corner, there were more pirates than we had anticipated. "Peter, Peter," I cried. "Do something. The pirates are coming closer, and we're out of ammunition!" My nine-year-old captain stood erect and said, "Don't worry, Mama." Pointing his plastic sword at them, he shouted the message of Isaiah 54:17: "No weapon formed against us will prosper!"

Storing God's Word in your child's heart at a young age is the most important parental responsibility and takes less than five minutes per day.

SOCIAL TRAINING

Children and teens who know what to expect possess confidence and know to respond in social environments. So at a young age teach them how to look directly into an adult's eyes, shake their hands, and smile. Practice this before an adult event as you teach them how to say the person's name and to ask about his or her family. This also instills an important "the sun-doesn't-rise-and-set-around-you" message.

Twice a year fifteen mostly pastoral couples from the TBI Board of Regents came to our home. A week before they arrived, I put their pictures on the refrigerator to familiarize the kids with them. After they learned a few names, I would tell the kids funny things about them so they wouldn't get intimidated by the adults. Sitting on the boys' Bert and Ernie beds, I would say, "Tomorrow some of our board is coming over, and they will probably say, 'How are you?'

Let's think of one thing you've been busy with, so you can answer their question in a super cool way." We would decide whether they should talk their new keyboard, G.I. Joe collection, or princess party. The next day all three were primed and drew positive affirmation from talking to adults.

Social training includes helping children learn to channel their emotions. While you shouldn't tolerate emotional outbursts, remember your objective is to direct instead of correct. If one of our children wouldn't respond to a "good morning" greeting at breakfast, I sent them back to their room to try again. I granted them grace if they felt grumpy or were worried about a test, but I taught them that as a family we do not ignore one another.

Although Andrew was an even-tempered guy with a long fuse, two of his emotional explosions could have turned sour had I not waited for the Holy Spirit to guide me. Due to some academic issues, I homeschooled him from fifth through eighth grade. One day in a moment of exasperation, he threw a book against the wall and said, "I hate science." Though blindsided by his frustration, I whispered, "Andrew, I hate science too. Let's go for a bike ride." That night we laughed about it, and I was grateful that I responded to his frustration instead of overreacting to his words.

At sixteen, Andrew overheard some hypocritical statements among the staff and watched a leader he greatly admired unjustly take credit for a success. For several months I watched his heart harden. One night at dinner he snapped, "I don't even know if I believe what you and Dad believe anymore." Since Tommy was away, Andrew and his two younger siblings waited for my response. They were stunned when I nonchalantly said, "Andrew, I'm sure proud of you. You're realizing that you can no longer live by your parents' convictions. You're gonna have to develop your own core values. Just analyze everything by God's Word and not people's opinions." I saw three jaws wide open. No sermon or condemnation, just permission to walk out their own salvation.

By the way, before you think raising three kids at a Christian camp guaranteed that they would love God, I rescued them a jillion times from older kids hooked on pornography and impatient staff who shoved them into a corner or tried to use them to get a raise. Not to mention that they had to constantly share their parents with other people's dysfunctional children. Parents, even if you are living in a convent, make your household your first priority. The grace of God and involved parents' faithful diligence produce great children.

There is no junior Holy Spirit: Andrew at age eight and at twenty

No High Like the Most High

Do whatever it takes to get your children involved in a church where they can get positive peer pressure and regularly experience God's presence. When they see there is no high like the Most High, they will crave their eternal destiny. All three of our children attended Columbus public schools, where they tried soccer, karate, ballet, Scouts, football, track, and twirling. But nothing gave them as much purpose and self-respect as serving God at Discovery Camp. They had to plow through expectations others tried to place on them yet stay focused on developing their God-given gifts. Teenagers need permission to be periodically grumpy, messy, and normal. Ours faced so many unrealistic expectations that I intentionally ignored the occasional missed curfew or ketchup stains on a new shirt.

Likewise, parents reading this might feel concerned about a child's negative choices or an adult child who has strayed from the Lord. If you have done everything you knew to do and your child is stuck on stupid, keep clinging to God's promises, such as: "He is God, the faithful God who keeps covenant and mercy for a thousand generations" (Deut. 7:9) and "The posterity of the righteous will be delivered" (Prov. 11:21). I know a mother whose twentysomething was flipping motorcycles and exhibiting other out-of-control behavior. The Holy Spirit promised her, "Until My wisdom abides in him, My mercy will hover over him." Today he leads a great ministry. Isaiah said that the children the Lord gave him were for signs and wonders. So are yours!

Trust in the Word of God that is inside your son or daughter because that Word never returns empty. Though I have mentioned this verse before, its reassurance bears repeating: "He who has begun a good work in [them] will complete it" (Phil. 1:6). Against all odds, Tommy and I have watched thousands of gospel-hardened young people melt in the presence of God's great love. And that, my praying parent, can happen late one night as your child gazes into a starlit sky or hears a song that softens his heart. It is amazing what God can do—all by Himself!

THE MIRACLE OF FAMILY

Success in marriage consists not only in finding the right mate, but being the right mate.

—Dwight L. Moody[3]

No, I've never thought of divorce in all these thirty-five years of marriage, but I did think of murder a few times.

—Ruth Bell Graham[4]

Marriage is not about competing, but completing.

—Dr. Myles Munroe[5]

Children are like wet cement. Whatever falls on them makes an impression.

—Dr. Haim Ginott, renowned family psychologist[6]

The family: It is an ever-changing mobile of life...a center for the formation of human relationships...a perpetual relayer of truth...a museum of memories.

—Edith Schaeffer[7]

CHAPTER 12

Go Ye, but Stay Put

⁊ **Life Question:** What is the secret for long-term success?

⁊ **Miracle Moment:** The miracle of steadfastness

⁊ **Life Lesson:** Live this day with that Day in your heart.

SOME TWENTY-FIVE YEARS AFTER WE OPENED DISCOVERY CAMP, our lives continue to be a revolving door of chartered buses, church vans, and parent-driven Suburbans. All come bringing campers who are searching for truth and leave overwhelmed by the goodness of God. Miracle moments have occurred at every turn of these memorable years. For that we are deeply grateful. Through the dedication of our awesome staff and Tommy's strong leadership, we have built a Christian conference center and a Bible school. Wouldn't you think that would keep us busy enough? Apparently not.

Before we got engaged, Tommy told me, "I dearly love you, but God has called me to pastor, so we cannot continue this relationship unless you're comfortable with being a pastor's wife." Well, love is blind. I wouldn't have cared if he had said that God called us to do the laundry for everyone in China. Every few years he would mention planting a church, but he was such a father in the faith at our camps I assumed that was sufficient. Then, without warning, I heard a strange expression in my spirit: "Go ye, but stay put." It proved to be a needed word for our next assignment. On January 24, 2005, the Holy Spirit awakened me at 3:03 a.m. (there I go tracking early-morning wake-up times again) to find Tommy entranced in a six-hour-long, heavenly visitation. The presence of angels filled our home, leaving us speechless. The Lord thundered, "I'll gather an army of believers around this voice of faith. It will be a church filled with My love, My Word, and My power. Miracles will be commonplace, and a thousand missionaries will be joined to your heart."

In September of 2006 Dr. T. L. Osborn, our dear friend and mentor, dedicated Believers World Outreach Church in Katy, Texas. Over the next six years we purchased pristine land off Interstate 10 and completed the first phase without incurring any debt. We did this during a declining economy and without taking one special offering. Each Sunday the most awesome body of believers a pastor ever could hope for declares, "We are believers. That's who we are. That's what we do." We are passionately committed to helping people find their place in Christ, raise their families, and nurture their marriages.

First a camp and Bible school, now a church

Forty miles to the west at our camp, that prophetic "Go ye, but stay put" word I had received steadied our staff. As understanding of our new assignment unfolded, God assured us that saying "hello" to the church did not require us to say "good-bye" to the camp. Tommy explained to staff members that the church didn't compete with our vision; it completed it. The cloud didn't move; it expanded. How exciting! Nevertheless, as the vision moved forward, we also had to look out the back window and deal with increasing camp maintenance. Our two-decade-old equipment and buildings needed constant repair. So did our dear staff, who had attempted to squeeze their family lives into a calendar of endless activities.

Shepherds don't drive their sheep; they guide them. We needed to lead our staff to some still waters. So we adjusted schedules, and within several months, the sheep were happy again. While a long-term commitment to keep the camp strong required costly repairs and renovations, we wanted it to outlive us. Success without a successor is failure. Whether a person or a committee, legacy is intentional. Think beyond your own lifetime and make some adjustments so your influence will also reach into generations yet to come.

STICKABILITY

To not get tempted by something new, flashy, and exciting, you will need what I call "stickability." Do you know people who change jobs, churches, or (God forbid) spouses every few years? Jesus did say "Go ye therefore" (Matt. 28:19, KJV), but once you arrive, you need to "stay put" long enough to complete a task. Everyone faces the temptation to "go ye" every time we face discouragement, disillusionment, or weariness. You might be certain that the grass is greener somewhere else, but rest assured, they have brown patches too. If you will water your brown patches, green pastures will return. Much to the dismay of you "cruise-a-matics," keeping a vision strong requires mundane, day-to-day maintenance.

At work, don't move every time your employer neglects to acknowledge your project or contributions. Don't change churches every time your pastor serves some spiritual veggies instead of letting you shout over the whipped cream. Stay put. Settle in. Hunker down. Don't compete, complain, or compare. That "new thing" a prophet mentioned is not a geographical move, but a spiritual awakening that is happening *in you, for you,* and *through you.* Be part of a team building something into the next generation. Learn to attack each day with the strength of a sprinter and each year with a marathon mind-set. As we stand on the shoulders of those who have gone on before us, we must recognize that life is not only a sprint or a marathon but also a relay. I believe that today we are running the last leg and the baton is in the church's hand.

Keep On Keepin' On

Although Tommy and I have received national recognition for Discovery Camp's success, we are quick to acknowledge the invaluable role played by our dedicated staff. While the grace on that original team to build the camp inspired us, the commitment of today's team to keep it strong is even greater.

It takes two types of people working together to fulfill the purposes of God. They are graced with different motivations yet connected to the same cause. (Aesop's fable of the "Tortoise and the Hare" could apply here.[1]) The corporate world labels these two types "Type A" or "Type B" personalities, or builders or maintainers, but I call them pioneers or settlers. The pioneers hear, "Go ye," while the settlers hear, "Stay put." The pioneers hear, "Get out of the boat," while the settlers hear, "Steady the boat." The pioneers hear, "Push on and build," while the settlers hear, "Settle in and maintain." The pioneers hear, "Make it happen," while the settlers hear, "Keep it going." A vision requires both the inspiration and perspiration of pioneers and settlers to sustain the dream.

WHEN WEARINESS SETS IN

As the years pass, it isn't that you don't love the Lord anymore or recognize His works in your ministry, family, or business. Yet after a few decades you may just get tired of some of the "stuff" that goes with it. You know what I mean—the boring, clock-in-and-clock-out rut called routine. Everyone faces it: the never-ending maintenance or tedious tasks required to nail that contract. Leaders get weary of inspiring their team, secretaries face endless stacks of data, salesmen bang out numbers that are *never quite good enough*, and homemakers wonder if there's a bottom to their laundry baskets. This is not a physical weariness but an emotionally draining parasite in our souls.

Weariness occurs when the vision gets muddied by the mundane. Don't get discouraged. Commitment to those mundane and tedious tasks keeps the wheels turning. Many formerly successful businesses and ministries have failed to continue due to a lack of understanding this one principle: it is the day-to-day mundane in a ministry that sustains the miracles, in the same way the mundane in a business creates profits. This is why you must be on guard against weariness. It invites poor judgment. Have you known the adrenaline rush of being the winner and achieving number-one status? Being surrounded by applause and admiration has an addictive element, doesn't it?

David experienced this elation as a fifteen-year-old kid when he took down the nine-foot giant Goliath.[2] He stared daily at Goliath's huge sword, which hung as a trophy in his tent. Ah, those were the good ol' days. However, as the years passed things changed dramatically. Jealous King Saul attempted to kill David at least ten times[3]; some Bible scholars cite twenty-one assassination attempts.[4] Eight years of living a fugitive's life and sleeping in caves grew old.[5] And who lived in those caves? David's unsolicited army: four hundred men in debt, distress, and discontentment. (See 1 Samuel 22:2.) What a party that wasn't!

"It's just a matter of time until Saul murders me," David moaned, "and I'm so weary of being hunted like an animal." Weariness made David vulnerable to poor judgment, prompting him to declare, "Enough is enough. Men, it's time to move to safer land. We'll leave tomorrow for Philistine country and find safety among King Achish and his people." They lived there for sixteen months, out of the will of God, and were subject to many unnecessary woes. (See 1 Samuel 27; 29–30).

STEADY IS THE NEW STRONG

One time on a visit a ministry partner asked, "What's your secret? How do you guys just keep on keepin' on?" He was fishing for a formula that could help him survive his company's collapse, but I responded with one word: steadfastness. Two of my favorite scriptures speak to this:

- "And let us not be weary in well doing: for in due season we shall reap, *if we faint not*" (Gal. 6:9, KJV, emphasis added).

- "Therefore my beloved brethren, be steadfast, immovable, always abounding in the work of the Lord, knowing that your labor is not in vain in the Lord" (1 Cor. 15:58).

Steadfastness is the determination to remain immovable and firm in belief and not be subject to change. Here are some word pictures: linebacker, ox, bulldozer. Steadfast people have backbones of iron that are anchored in concrete. They roll up their sleeves and move full steam ahead toward a fixed goal while ignoring distractions. There are no goose bumps or glory clouds; just a job to do for the Jesus they love.

The future Believers World Outreach Church

STEADFASTNESS REDIRECTS DISCOURAGEMENT

Steadfastness helps strengthen you amid the relentless demands of maintaining a ministry or family business. We know how overwhelming it can get. Even the apostle Paul wrote of the obstacles on one journey and how "our bodies had no rest, but we were troubled on every side. Outside were conflicts, inside were fears" (2 Cor. 7:5). It takes steadfastness to push through that daunting type of discouragement. During David's "out of God's will" season, the Amalekites burned the city of Ziklag and took the wives and children captive: "Now David was greatly distressed, for the people spoke of stoning him, because the soul of all the people was grieved, every man for his sons and his daughters. But David strengthened himself in the LORD his God" (1 Sam. 30:6).

Sometimes when you feel as though the entire world has turned against you, you wonder if things could get any worse. In David's case, his world really had turned against him. He sank to his lowest moment, feeling the burden of the men's loss, the trauma of his personal pain, and—in his gut—knowing he bore responsibility for trekking his men away from God's land, Israel. His spiritual response revealed his inner strength. As impressive as that is, how do you do that when you feel, as we say in Texas, "lower than a snake's belly"? If you will steadfastly do these three things, courage will return:

1. Remember past victories.

2. Offer a sacrifice of praise.

3. Pray in the Holy Spirit.

Steadfastness helps redirect your spiritual senses and focus you on "that" day. Seeing the bigger picture can reduce life's triviality to this reality—there are only two days in life that really matter: *this* day and *that* Day. On *that* Day all of humanity will stand before their Creator to give an account for their choices. Those who rejected Jesus Christ as their Savior will stand before the great white throne (described in Revelation 20:11) and receive the sentence of eternal death, separating them from God forever. Those who trusted in the shed blood of Jesus Christ for their salvation will stand before the judgment seat of Christ to receive His welcoming smile and eternal rewards. As believers, we live *this* day with *that* Day in our hearts. Here are a few of the many Bible references that confirm that wonderful day when we see Him face-to-face:

+ Romans 14:10: *All believers will stand before the judgment seat of Christ.*

+ Romans 14:12: *All believers will give an account of themselves to God.*

+ 1 Corinthians 1:8: *Grace will make you blameless in that Day.*

+ 1 Corinthians 3:13: *That Day will reveal any works or motives not founded on Christ.*

- 2 Corinthians 5:10: *All believers receive the things done in the body, whether good or bad.*

- 2 Timothy 1:12: *He can keep what you commit to Him until that Day.*

- 2 Timothy 1:18: *On that Day God will give mercy to believers who ministered to other believers.*

- 2 Timothy 4:8: *Believers will receive a crown of righteousness.*

- Hebrews 10:25: *Don't neglect Christian fellowship because that Day is approaching.*

Those who understand the serious ramifications of *that* Day will live with pure motives and proper priorities. Steadfastness causes you to focus on the prize, not the price. To get a better picture of that Day, imagine a four-inch sausage patty tossed into a frying pan. As the fire ignites, it shrinks the sausage to half its original size as everything artificial gets burned off. Likewise on that Day, one flash of being in His presence will burn off everything in our lives that is not pure. Whatever is left will be rewarded. It is quite possible that a stay-at-home mom who organized a food program for shut-ins will receive more rewards than a carnal evangelist. We both shudder and shine at the very thought of it.

STEADFASTNESS BRINGS REWARDS

The rewards for a steadfast life are not just for the sweet by-and-by. You can expect them in the nasty now-and-now. Part of your Earthly Reward Program includes the joy of knowing your life has eternal significance, as well as peace during difficult moments. Another reward, recorded in Acts 16:31, is the promise of your household's salvation. The Lord wants to assure you that as you pour your life into reaching His family, He will cause others to reach your family. His "thank-yous" are simply awesome!

Whether their staff are volunteers or salaried, employers who are blessed with a team of supportive workers should provide the highest level of earthly rewards possible. Our goal is to provide our employees with an equal or higher benefit package than they would receive at a comparable occupation in the secular world. In addition to their compensation, our staff enjoys no-cost housing, quality health insurance, and paid vacations. Many of our ministry positions include vehicles, laptops, and cell phones. Why wouldn't we bless our staff this way? People who have canceled vacations, shared holidays with strangers, and been on-call round-the-clock for twenty-five years deserve appropriate thanks. They provide the muscle behind the miracles.

We are eternally indebted to those who have served with us for so long. Each one in his or her heart has counted the cost of joining something bigger than self. They don't need continual pats on the back to keep them focused. Not only does their steadfastness inspire me daily, but I also rejoice in knowing they will receive phenomenal eternal rewards. So will other wonderful staff who served and sowed with us for several years before moving on to other fields of service.

FIVE CROWNS IN HEAVEN

While you cannot earn your salvation, once you have accepted Christ and are born again, the great rewarder longs to say "thank you." The New Testament mentions many eternal rewards, among them five crowns. We have no reason to question whether they are literal; apparently they will function as a distinction of honor. Revelation 4:10 says that the twenty-four elders will lay their crowns down at His feet, so I'm sure we will too. These crowns include:

1. The crown of righteousness for those who are waiting for the return of the Lord Jesus Christ: "There is laid up for me the crown of righteousness, which the Lord, the righteous Judge, will give to me on that Day, and not to me only but also to all who have loved His appearing" (2 Tim. 4:8).

2. The victor's crown for those who disciplined their bodies and brought them under subjection, demonstrating self-control: "Now they do it to obtain a perishable crown, but we for an imperishable crown. Therefore I run thus: not with uncertainty. Thus I fight: not as one who beats the air. But I discipline my body and bring it into subjection, lest, when I have preached to others, I myself should become disqualified" (1 Cor. 9:25–27).

3. The crown of life for those who endured patiently through trials or were faithful even unto death: "Indeed, the devil is about to throw some of you into prison, that you may be tested, and you will have tribulation ten days. Be faithful until death, and I will give you the crown of life" (Rev. 2:10).

4. The crown of glory to godly leaders who served as examples to people entrusted to their care: "Shepherd the flock of God which is among you, serving as overseers, not by compulsion but willingly, not for dishonest gain but eagerly; nor as being lords over those entrusted to you, but being examples to the flock; and when the Chief Shepherd appears, you will receive the crown of glory that does not fade away" (1 Pet. 5:2–4).

5. The crown of rejoicing (also known as the soulwinners' crown) for believers who obeyed the great

commission: "For what is our hope, or joy, or crown of rejoicing? Is it not even you in the presence of our Lord Jesus Christ at His coming? For you are our glory and joy" (1 Thess. 2:19–20).

Rest assured that the unseen one observes every good deed and will reward it appropriately. As Jesus said, "For whoever gives you a cup of water to drink in My name, because you belong to Christ, assuredly, I say to you, he will by no means lose his reward" (Mark 9:41). That puts our food service department, which serves 121,694 meals over ten weeks of summer camp, at the top of the list.

YOUR SECRET WEAPON

Speaking in tongues is a key weapon in a believer's arsenal that will keep you steadfast. It prevents weariness and releases supernatural sustenance. This precious prayer language gift is available to all spiritually thirsty believers. There is nothing spooky about speaking in tongues, which signifies your eternal spirit talking to God's Spirit. It is simply done in a spiritual language. I like to explain it to children this way: "In China they speak Chinese. In Japan they speak Japanese. When you speak in tongues, you are speaking Heavenese." People sometimes ask if they can be filled with the Holy Spirit but not ask for tongues. My reply: "I guess you could, but why would you not want Jesus's gift? Have you ever seen a pair of shoes without the accompanying tongues? So the tongues come with the Holy Spirit."

Speaking in tongues is an endless source of rest and refreshing. Paul, who wrote half of the New Testament, quoted this prophecy from Isaiah: "'This is the rest with which you may cause the weary to rest,' and, 'This is the refreshing'" (Isa. 28:12). Have you ever relaxed by a rippling river? As you pray in the Spirit, you are releasing rivers of living water within your being. Praying in the Spirit strengthens and reinforces your inner man and assures the release of God's will.

Every one of Jesus's disciples, including His birth mother, spoke in tongues. I will go on record as saying it wasn't a casual, ten-minute "she-ka-la" type of prayer on the way to work. No wonder the Jews of Thessalonica said, "These who have turned the world upside down have come here too" (Acts 17:6).

HIT IT WITH TONGUES!

In August of 1981 a group invited me to Belize for the sole purpose of ministering the baptism of the Holy Spirit to a group of influential Catholic women. Approximately three hundred gathered and listened to my explanation and concluding invitation: "Raise your hand if you'd like to receive this mighty baptism of the Holy Spirit." Not one hand raised. I reworded the invitation and repeated it. Still no hands. I asked silently, "Lord, what am I doing wrong? How can I reach these beautiful ladies?" He replied, "Invite them to experience what Mary received in that upper room." Bingo! Every sweet, brown hand went up, so I simply said, "Lift your other hand too and receive the Holy Spirit in the name of Jesus." Within five minutes the entire group was speaking in tongues.

Just like that group in Belize, people who speak in tongues daily don't burn out because the Holy Spirit continually stokes their spirit man's fire. If you will daily set aside time to pray in the Spirit, you will receive healing of chronic ailments, find long-sought answers, and have a zeal for the house of God. Extravagant resorts might refresh your soul and body, but praying in the Spirit refreshes your spirit. That's why Psalm 42:7 describes it as "deep calls to deep" (NIV). We knew of a powerful grandmother in East Texas whose prayers kept the world turning. She had the cutest expression when facing an important decision or a fiery dart: "Hit it with tongues, honey, hit it with tongues!" Many times we stop our busy world to "hit it with tongues," and without fail the answer arrives, whether in a dream, a *rhema* scripture, or a prophetic word.

SNOBBY CHARISMATICS

Speaking in tongues is not a badge to wear, as if it makes you superior to other brothers and sisters in Christ. If you act like that, shame on you! All Christians have a measure of the Holy Spirit abiding in them; the Spirit drew them to their salvation experience. I compare this to a happy little bottle bobbing in the ocean, singing, "I'm in the ocean. I'm in the ocean." When the force of a wave popped the bottle's cork off, it sank blub, blub, blub down into the water. His song changed as he sang, "The ocean's in me, the ocean's in me." Such is the difference between two genuine Christians who are (as I describe it) Spirit-filled or Spirit-spilled.

The New Testament explains two types of tongues. The first involves man speaking to God (your prayer language), and the second is God speaking to man (the gift of tongues). Your prayer language needs no interpretation because your spirit is talking to the Spirit of God, who understands everything. The gift of tongues needs to be interpreted by someone with the gift of interpretation. In referring to both types of tongues, Paul said (mostly my paraphrase), "Please follow the church guidelines, and keep order in your services, but *do not forbid to speak with tongues*" (1 Cor. 14:39).

COWBOY CADILLACS

Speaking in tongues keeps your spiritual tank full. Men in Texas seem to think that God's armor includes a pickup truck. They love, love, love their trucks. Tommy used to drive a noisy Ford F350 crew cab with dual gas tanks. He and our second son were on a two-hundred-mile road trip when eight-year-old Peter noticed they were almost out of gas. Noticing our son's concern, my fun-loving Tommy said, "Peter, there's no gas station for forty miles, but if you'll speak in tongues, your supernatural prayer language will put diesel in our tank." As Peter began to pray, Tommy reached down and flipped a switch under the dash, and a wide-eyed Peter watched the needle on the gas tank slowly move to "full." Although Peter was thrilled, Tommy had to admit his truck carried a reserve tank. The lesson: steadfast people learn to speak in tongues before they run empty and keep on praying so their secret tank stays full.

STEADFASTNESS SPOTLIGHTS JESUS

Just minutes before the scheduled opening curtain for a small church production titled "The Miracles of Jesus," word came that the spotlight operator had bailed out on the cast. The substitute, a junior high student, received one instruction: "Keep the spotlight on Jesus." No one thought to explain that he also bore responsibility for the house lights. The play began in the dark, yet the spotlight shone on Jesus. The drama director assumed that he would catch on, but the youth kept the spotlight on Jesus. Finally he sent a note to the junior high do-gooder, but since it was too dark to read, the youth kept the spotlight focused on Jesus. During the twenty-minute drama, Bartimaeus got healed and Peter walked on the water, both in the dark, as the spotlight remained on Jesus.

How do you "keep on keepin' on" and live a life of miracles? Keep the spotlight on Jesus. As Paul wrote to the Colossians, "And He is before all things, and in Him all things consist. And He is the head of the body, the church, who is the beginning, the firstborn from the dead, that in all things He may have the preeminence" (Col. 1:17–18). Indeed, Jesus promised that "if I am lifted up from the earth, I will draw all peoples to Myself" (John 12:32). Within every human being resides an eternal spirit longing for Jesus. Millions attempt to fill that longing with religion, relationships, addictions, or ambition, but He will continue to draw them to people like you and places like Discovery Camp as you steadfastly spotlight Jesus. He is the only One who rewards your steadfast routines. He is the only One who can take your mess and create a miracle.

THE ORIGIN OF PEARLS

Miracles remind me of pearls because of the way they are made. Once in Hong Kong I asked God to give me a husband with a big destiny. While there I also purchased a long strand of cultured pearls. I have worn them proudly for thirty-two years, never fully understanding how they were created. Most jewelry is fashioned out of precious metals and jewels that are found buried deep in the earth. However, pearls are found inside a living being, an oyster. Pearls represent the result of a biological process—the oyster's way of protecting itself from foreign substances. When an irritant enters the oyster's shell, it secretes a substance called "nacre" to encapsulate it, thus creating a pearl.[6] The oyster's appropriate response to pain produces a pearl. I find it humorous to think that I paid dearly for my beautiful strand of 125 pearls when they originated with 125 irritants.

Forgive this silly story, but let's consider Oscar the Oyster, my imaginary friend, displaying his five pearls at "Show-and-Tell Day" on the ocean's floor. Pointing at his first exhibit, Oscar proclaims, "This was my first pearl. It began at a murky moment when sand intruded into my house. Ouch!" Moving to his second exhibit, Oscar explains, "This next pearl was created when a tiny piece of rock got under my skin. Ugh!" Moving to his largest pearl with great enthusiasm, Oscar exclaims, "My! My! Here is my favorite pearl and my greatest trophy! I survived an invasion of a nasty parasite called a Nematode worm. It almost destroyed me, but I was determined to overcome and continued to secrete my nacre. Every time that it rubbed me wrong, I squirted more of my secret solution to encapsulate it. It was a long five-year process, but it formed a beautiful pearl. Look at this gem now! Who would have ever thought that something so painful could become the beginning of something so beautiful?" Applause rippled through the waters, and Oscar the Oyster finished his presentation by offering seaweed Slurpees to his salty friends.

MY PEARL EPIPHANY

These twelve life lessons learned from five hundred thousand campers over twenty-five years have become an invisible, multistrand necklace of pearls that I wear daily. Each pearl represents God's faithfulness to a network of churches, a praying parent, a wiggly child, or a searching teen. Strung tightly together are campers who have traveled two miles down a winding, country road onto an unimpressive pasture and slept in bunk beds crammed into metal dorms, only to find the unsearchable riches of Christ.

This book has been about the Discovery Camp story, but your life is also like a string of pearls. Each represents a miracle moment when Jesus became your Savior then your Master, your Counselor, and your Friend. Pearl by pearl, you remember a time of darkness when He was your Light, or the mercy of your loving Shepherd when you strayed. Even today He can be the Healer of your broken heart, broken life, or broken body. Your miracle moments are strung together by His matchless love. Do not attempt to select your favorite miracle, because it is still yet to come. The ultimate miracle moment, to which there is no worthy competitor, will occur when you leave your "oyster" shell behind and you hear Him say, "'Well done, good and faithful servant; you were faithful over a few things, I will make you ruler over many things. Enter into the joy of your lord'" (Matt. 25:21). When you lay your pearls down before the Pearl of Great Price, it will mark the beginning of your eternity of miracle moments.

THE MIRACLE OF STEADFASTNESS

Stickability is 95 percent of ability.

—David J. Schwartz[7]

Even a mosquito doesn't get a slap on the back until the work is done.

—Anonymous[8]

There is no substitute for hard work.

—Thomas Edison[9]

It's not that I'm so smart, it's just that I stay with problems longer.

—Albert Einstein[10]

The will to persevere is often the difference between failure and success.

—David Sarnoff, NBC founder[11]

Whether you think you can or you think you can't, you are right.

—Henry Ford[12]

With men this is impossible,
but with God all things are possible.

—Matthew 19:26

Notes

CHAPTER 1—GOD'S PERFECT TIMING

1. "Jesus Loves Me" by Anna Bartlett Warner. Public domain.

2. J. Gilchrist Lawson, "George Müller," Christian Biography Resources, http://www.wholesomewords.org/biography/bmuller2.html (accessed January 21, 2013).

3. "Turn Your Eyes Upon Jesus" by Helen Lemmel. Public domain.

4. WorldForge, "The Life of an Eagle," http://www.worldforge.org/dev/systems/soar/rules/life (accessed January 21, 2013).

5. Rev. Seaton D. Wilson, *Soar Like an Eagle, Reign Like a King* (Bloomington, IN: CrossBooks, 2010), 28–54, 61–63.

6. Author personally heard John Osteen say this in a sermon. Used by permission, Lakewood Church in Houston, Texas.

7. ThinkExist.com, "Peter Marshall Quotes," http://thinkexist.com/quotation/teach_us_o_lord_the_disciplines_of_patience-for/11728.html (accessed January 21, 2013).

8. GoodReads.com, "Elisabeth Elliot Quotes," http://www.goodreads.com/quotes/360361-i-realized-that-the-deepest-spiritual-lessons-are-not-learned (accessed January 21, 2013).

CHAPTER 2—THE BIG MOVE

1. W. T. Purkiser, editor, C. E. Demaray, Donald S. Metz, Maude A. Stuneck, *Exploring the Old Testament* (Kansas City, MO: Beacon Hill Press, 1955), 128.

2. Frank Charles Thompson, *Thompson Chain Reference Bible* (Indianapolis, IN: Kirkbridge Bible Co., Inc., 1988), map 6.

3. Don Gossett and E. W. Kenyon, *The Power of Your Words* (New Kensington, PA: Whitaker House, 1977), 46.

4. Alan Richardson and John Bowden, editors, *The Westminster Dictionary of Christian Theology* (Philadelphia, PA: The Westminster Press, 1983), 545.

5. Benjamin Franklin, *Poor Richard's Almanack* (Waterloo, IA: The U. S. C. Publishing Co., 1914), 52. Viewed at Google Books.

6. BrainyQuote, http://www.brainyquote.com/quotes/quotes/s/saintaugus121380.html (accessed February 19, 2013).

7. E. W. Kenyon, *What Happened From the Cross to the Throne* (Lynwood, WA: Kenyon's Gospel Publishing Society, 1998), 156.

8. Charles Capps, *The Tongue: A Creative Force* (Tulsa, OK: Harrison House, Inc., 1976).

9. BrainyQuote, http://www.brainyquote.com/quotes/quotes/p/plato159576.html (accessed February 19, 2013).

CHAPTER 3—GOD FULFILLS VISION

1. JustDisney.com, "Disneyland History," http://www.justdisney.com/disneyland/history.html (accessed January 25, 2013).

2. Pat Groce & Company, "Eye on Entrepreneur: Be a Vision Keeper," http/www.patcroce.com/entrepreneur/keeper.html (accessed January 25, 2013).

3. Finis Jennings Dake, *Dake's Annotated Reference Bible* (Lawerenceville, GA: Dake's Bible Sales, 1963).

4. *God's Plowman: The Story of Henry Krause* (Los Angeles: Full Gospel Businessmen's Fellowship International, 1966), 30–35.

5. ThinkExist.com, "John C. Maxwell Quotes," http://thinkexist.com/quotation/a-great-leader-s-courage-to-fulfill-his-vision/761530.html (accessed January 25, 2013).

6. Paul Sloane, "How to Develop a Vision for Innovation," http://www.innovationtools.com/Articles/EnterpriseDetails.asp?a=455 (accessed January 25, 2013).

7. ThinkExist.com, "Edwin Markham Quotes," http://thinkexist.com/quotation/the_crest_and_crowning_of_all_good-life-s_final/205410.html (accessed January 25, 2013).

8. Bob Phillips, *Phillips' Book Great Thoughts Funny Sayings* (Carol Stream, IL: Tyndale House Publishers, Inc., 1993), 101.

9. Tommy Burchfield, "Seven Ways to Nurture Your Vision," *Signs & Wonders Today*, May 1996.

10. LeadershipNow, "Quotes on Vision," http://www.leadershipnow.com/visionquotes.html (accessed February 19, 2013).

11. Van Crouch, *Winning 101: Insight and Motivation to Help You Achieve Excellence* (Tulsa, OK: Honor Books, 1995), 74.

12. Wayne Myers, *Truth in a Nutshell* (Dallas: Wayne Myers, The Great Commission Evangelistic Association, 2008), 32.

CHAPTER 4—SUICIDES AND SETBACKS

1. Wikipedia, "Hurricane Katrina," http://en.wikipedia.org/wiki/Hurricane_Katrina (accessed January 28, 2013).

2. PBS Newshour, "Hurricane Katrina Displaced 400,000 Gulf Coast Residents, Report Says," http://www.pbs.org/newshour/updates/social_issues/jan-june06/census_06-07.html3 (accessed January 28, 2013).

3. The author personally heard this interview.

4. Elisabeth Elliot, "Radio Broadcasts," http://www.elisabethelliot.org/radio.html (accessed January 28, 2013).

5. Max Lucado, *Hope Pure and Simple* (Nashville: Thomas Nelson, 2007), 30.

6. BrainyQuote, http://www.brainyquote.com/quotes/authors/t/tertullian.html (accessed February 19, 2013).

7. Beliefnet, "Inspirational Quotes," http://www.beliefnet.com/Quotes/Christian/C/Catherine-Marshall/God-Is-The-Only-One-Who-Can-Make-The-Valley-Of-Tro.aspx (accessed February 19, 2013).

8. BrainyQuote, http://www.brainyquote.com/quotes/quotes/b/billygraha150656.html (accessed February 19, 2013).

9. Tertullian, *Apologeticum (The Apology)*, Tertulian.org, http://www.tertullian.org/works/apologeticum.htm (accessed February 19, 2013).

CHAPTER 5—THE MIRACLE MESSAGE

1. Oral Roberts, *Christ in Every Book of the Bible* (Tulsa, OK: Pinoak Publications, 1975). Permission requested.

2. Nevin, Alfred, ed., et al. "Names, Titles and Characteristics of the Son of God, Jesus Christ Our Lord," The Parallel Bible, Blue Letter Bible, <http://blueletterbible.org/study/parallel/paral19.cfm> (accesed February 5, 2013).

3. Osborn.com, "About: Dr. T. L. Osborn," http://www.osborn.org/site/sections/12 (accessed January 28, 2013).

4. Brainy Quotes, "Francis of Assisi Quotes," http://www.brainyquote.com/quotes/authors/f/francis_of_assisi.html (accessed January 28, 2013).

5. Charles Stanley, *The Glorious Journey* (Nashville: Thomas Nelson Publishers, 1996), 426.

6. T. L. Osborn, *Soulwinning,* (Tulsa, OK: Osborn Publishers, 1963), 33.

7. Leonard Sweet and Frank Viola, *Jesus Manifesto* (Nashville: Thomas Nelson, 2010), 11.

8. Tony Evans, *Theology You Can Count On* (Chicago: Moody Publishers, 2009).

CHAPTER 6—GOD HASN'T LOST HIS RECIPE FOR MANNA

1. James Strong, *Strong's Exhaustive Concordance of the Bible* (Nashville: Abingdon Press, 1890), 452.

2. Beliefnet, "Inspirtational Quotes," http://www.beliefnet.com/Quotes/Evangelical/H/Hudson-Taylor/Gods-Work-Done-In-Gods-Way-Will-Never-Lack-Gods.aspx (accessed February 19, 2013).

3. Myers, *Truth in a Nutshell*, 60.

4. Tommy Burchfield, "Prosperity With a Purpose," *Signs & Wonders Today*, September 2002.

5. Myers, *Truth in a Nutshell*, 48.

CHAPTER 7—NO HIGH LIKE THE MOST HIGH

1. Fuchsia Pickett, *Understanding the Personality of the Holy Spirit* (Lake Mary, FL: Charisma House, 2004), 41–62.

2. H. Wayne House, *Chronological and Background Charts of the New Testament* (Grand Rapids, MI: Zondervan, 1981), 113.

3. Arthur Wallis, *Pray in the Spirit* (Ft. Washington, PA: Christian Literature Crusade, 1970), 104.

4. Sweet and Viola, *Jesus Manifesto*, 4.

5. Rachel Burchfield, "Understanding the Anointing," *Signs & Wonders Today*, March 1998.

6. Bill Johnson, *Face to Face With God* (Lake Mary, FL: Charisma House, 2007), 76.

CHAPTER 8—BEDPANS AND BULLDOZERS

1. ThinkExist.com, "Winston Churchill Quotes," http://thinkexist .com/quotation/attitude_is_a_little_thing_that_makes_a_big/219106 .html (accessed January 28, 2013).

2. Laboratory of Neuro Imaging, "Brain Trivia," http://www.loni.ucla .edu/About_Loni/education/brain_trivia.shtml (accessed January 28, 2013).

3. Brainy Quote, "Corrie ten Boom Quotes," http://www.brainyquote .com/quotes/authors/c/corrie_ten_boom.html (accessed January 29, 2013).

4. ThinkExist.com, "Thomas Babington Macaulay Quotes," http:// thinkexist.com/quotes/thomas_babington_macaulay/ (accessed January 28, 2013).

5. Goodreads.com, "Lao Tzu Quotable Quotes," http://www .goodreads.com/quotes/217207-watch-your-thoughts-they-become-words -watch-your-words-they (accessed January 28, 2013).

6. Brainy Quote, "Horace Greeley Quotes," http://www.brainyquote .com/quotes/quotes/h/horacegree150676.html (accessed January 28, 2013).

7. Brainy Quote, "Thomas Paine Quotes," http://www.brainyquote.com/ quotes/quotes/t/thomaspain106084.html (accessed January 28, 2013).

CHAPTER 9—N-O-T-T-M-M!

1. Pastyme With Good Companye, "Emperor Menelik II—Biblical Medicine," http://pastyme.uppercanadianheritage.com/index.php/emperor_ menelik_ii_biblical_medicine (accessed February 19, 2013); Geoffrey Regan, *Let Them Eat Cake* (London: Robson Books, 2003).

2. Eyewitness to History, "The California Gold Rush, 1849," http://www.eyewitnesstohistory.com/californiagoldrush.htm (accessed January 28, 2013).

3. Richard Booker, *Come and Dine* (Shippensburg, PA: Destiny Image, 1983), 98; Rachel Burchfield, *Texas Bible Institute Foundations for Life: How to Study Your Bible* (San Antonio, TX: Lebco Printing Company, n.d.), 79.

4. Kenneth E. Hagin, *The Believer's Authority* (Tulsa, OK: Kenneth Hagin Ministires, 1967).

5. E. W. Kenyon, *Father and His Family* (Lynwood, WA: Kenyon's Gospel Publishing Society, 1989).

6. Josh McDowell, *The New Evidence That Demands a Verdict* (Nashville: Thomas Nelson Publishers, 1999), 34.

7. Frances Ward, *Keep the Fruit on the Table* (Houston: n.p., 1976).

8. Billy Graham, "Our Bible," *Decision Magazine,* http://www.billygraham.org/articlepage.asp?articleid=691 (accessed February 19, 2013).

9. Myers, *Truth in a Nutshell,* 204.

CHAPTER 10—MANY SONS AND DAUGHTERS

1. GoodReads.com, "Mother Teresa Quotes," http://www.goodreads.com/author/quotes/838305mother_teresa (accessed January 29, 2013).

2. National Highway Traffic Safety Administration, "Research on Drowsy Driving," http://www.nhtsa.gov/Driving+Safety/Distracted+Driving/Research+on+Drowsy+Driving (accessed January 29, 2013).

3. Charles Stanley, *The Glorious Journey* (Nashville: Thomas Nelson Publishers, 1996), 463.

4. Wheaton.edu, "Jim Elliot Quote," Billy Graham Center, http://www2.wheaton.edu/bgc/archives/faq/20.htm (accessed February 20, 2013).

5. Walter A. Henrichsen, *Disciples Are Made, Not Born* (Colorado Springs, CO: Victor/Cook Communications, 1974).

6. Crouch, *Winning 101,* 86.

CHAPTER 11—GOD'S PLAN IS FAMILY

1. Goodreads.com, "C. S. Lewis Quotes," http://www.goodreads.com/quotes/20606-the-homemaker-has-the-ultimate-career-all-other-careers-exist (accessed January 29, 2013).

2. Ruth Bell Graham as quoted in Catherine Palmer and Gary Chapman, *Falling for You Again* (Carol Stream, IL: Tyndale House Publishers, Inc., 2007). Viewed at Google Books online.

3. Crouch, *Winning 101,* 122.

4. Search Quotes, "Ruth Graham Quotes," www.searchquotes.com/search/Ruth_Graham/ (accessed February 20, 2013).

5. Myles Munroe, *Keys for Marriage* (New Kensington, PA: Whitaker House, 1999), 141.

6. Haim Ginott, *Between Parent and Child* (New York: Macmillan, 1965).

7. L'Abri, http://www.labri.org/swiss/resource/edith.html (accessed February 20, 2013).

CHAPTER 12—GO YE, BUT STAY PUT

1. *Aesop's Fables*, retold by Joseph Jacobs, The Harvard Classics series, edited by Charles W. Eliot, (New York: P. F. Collier & Son, 1909–1914).

2. The Interactive Bible, http://tinyurl.com/auatsyv (accessed January 30, 2013).

3. WikiAnswers.com, http://wiki.answers.com/Q/How_many_times_did_saul_try_to_kill_david (accessed January 30, 2013).

4. Dake, *Dake's Annotated Reference Bible*.

5. The Interactive Bible, "Saul Hunts David," http://tinyurl.com/b9vbfwu (accessed January 30, 2013).

6. Costello's, "About Pearls," http://www.costellos.com.au/pearls/index2.html (accessed January 29, 2013).

7. David J. Schwartz, *The Magic of Thinking Big* (New York: Simon & Schuster, 1965), 35.

8. Myers, *Truth in a Nutshell*, 189.

9. Values.com, "Inspirational Quotes About Hard Work," http://www.values.com/inspirational-quotes/value/24--Hard-Work (accessed February 20, 2013).

10. Values.com, "Inspirational Quotes—Responsibility Quotes," http://www.values.com/inspirational-quotes/tag/responsibility-quotes?page=2 (accessed February 20, 2013).

11. ThinkExist.com, "David Sarnoff Quotes," http://thinkexist.com/quotation/the_will_to_persevere_is_often_the_difference/170053.html (accessed February 20, 2013).

12. Cool Quotes Collection, http://www.coolquotescollection.com/Wisdom/62 (accessed February 20, 2013).